The Edwards/Scott Family History

Edinburgh to Philadelphia

The Edwards/Scott Family History

Edinburgh to Philadelphia

Kathryn Chambers Torpey
Alexandria, Virginia

Kathryn Chambers Torpey is a professional genealogist and researcher. She is certified by the Board for Certification of Genealogists[SM].

Other Books by Kathryn Chambers Torpey:

John Kennedy of County Donegal, Ulster, Ireland, and His Descendants - A Compiled Genealogy (Including Risk, McCoy, and Pendleton), 2006

William Kennedy of Chester County, Pennsylvania, and His Descendants - A Compiled Genealogy (Including Davis, Smith, Wallace, Russell, and McClure), 2014

Colonial and Revolutionary Kennedy Families from Southeastern Pennsylvania, 2015

Imprint: CreateSpace Independent Publishing Platform

ISBN-13: 978-1530041091
ISBN-10: 1530041090

Torpey Books
5035 Domain Place
Alexandria, VA
22311-5066

In Memory of Annie Edwards Chambers

Had she been afforded an obituary, it may have read as follows:

On December 27, 1927, **ANNIE A. CHAMBERS** (nee Edwards), beloved wife of the late George W. Chambers, in the 80th year of her age. Survived by two sons, William S. Chambers and George E. Chambers, three daughters, Lydia E. Smith Roe, Emma C. Spence, and Annie I. Chambers, seven grandchildren and four great-grandchildren all of Philadelphia. Relatives and friends are invited to attend the funeral from the residence of her son-in-law, William Y. Spence, at 7119 Upland Street on December 31 at 9:00 A.M. To proceed to Mount Moriah Cemetery. Arrangements by E.B. Yerkes, 7031 Woodland Avenue.

Contents

INTRODUCTION. ix

DESCENDANT CHART FOR ADAM EDWARDS. xi

1. THE SCOTT FAMILY IN SCOTLAND. 1

    The Geography of the Borders and the Scottish Lowlands. 1
    The Origins of the Scottish Lowlanders. 1
    The Mind and Character of the Scottish Lowlander. 2
    County Selkirk (or Selkirkshire) Scotland. 2
    Selkirk - The Chief County Town. 2
    Galashiels - The Market-Town. 3
    County Roxburgh (or Roxburghshire), Scotland. 3

2. THE EDWARDS FAMILY IN SCOTLAND. 4

    Edinburgh, Midlothian (or Edinburghshire), Scotland. 4
    St. Cuthbert's Parish and Church. 4
        Edwards Family Marriages. 4
        Edwards Family Baptisms 5
    The New Towns of Edinburgh. 5
    Canonmills - The Flour-Milling Settlement. 6
    Employment, Trade and Manufacturing. 6
    Married Life in Edinburgh. 7
    The Edwards Family Bible. 8

3. THE EDWARDS FAMILY'S ARRIVAL IN AMERICA. 8

4. THE EDWARDS FAMILY IN AMERICA. 9

    Adam Edwards - Father. 9
    Joseph Campbell Edwards - The Youngest Son. 11
    Isabella (Scott) Edwards Flanagan - Mother. 11
        Marriage to Andrew Flanagan. 12
        The Death of Isabella (Scott) Edwards Flanagan. 12
        The Burial of Isabella (Scott) Edwards Flanagan. 13
        The Life and Times of Andrew Flanagan. 13
        The Death of Andrew Flanagan. 15
    George Edwards - The Oldest Son. 15
        Becoming A Citizen. 15
        Work History. 15
        Spring Garden Engine Company. 16

Marriage to Susan Brown. 16
Membership in Secret Societies. 16
The Death of George Edwards. 17
Dying Intestate. 17

Robert Edwards - The Surviving Twin.. 17
The Service in the Civil War. 17
The Naturalization of Robert Edwards.. 19
Marriage to Elizabeth Cusack. 20
Marriage to Rose Ann McFeely. 20
Marriage to Mary Dougherty 21
Work History 21
The Death of Robert Edwards 21

William Scott Edwards - The Civil War Veteran. 22
The Twenty-third Regiment 22
Becoming A Citizen 27
Applying for a Civil War Pension 27
Marriage to Jane Martin 27
Work History 28
The Death of Jane (Martin) Edwards 28
Marriage to Rose Clark 28
Married Life at 2502 Pine Street 29
Conversion to Roman Catholicism 29
Joining the Grand Army of the Republic 29
The Death of Rose (Clark) Edwards 29
The Death of William Scott Edwards 30
The Pennsylvania Memorial at Gettysburg 30

Annie Adam (Edwards) Chambers - The Only Daughter. 30
Marriage to George Washington Chambers 31
The Early Years 31
Wife and Mother 32
The Character of Annie Adam (Edwards) Chambers 34
Widowhood 34
The Death of Annie Adam (Edwards) Chambers 35

ENDNOTES 37

APPENDIX A - Possible Ancestors of Adam Edwards 57

APPENDIX B - Possible Ancestors of Isabella Scott 59

APPENDIX C - Deposition of Annie A. Chambers, June 3, 1910 61

APPENDIX D - Descendants of Adam Edwards. 63

INDEX 71

INTRODUCTION

This family history documents the life of Adam and Isabella (Scott) Edwards and their six children, George, William, Robert, Adam, Annie, and Joseph.

The first and second parts of the narrative describe the early history of the Scott and Edwards families in Scotland. The third part provides information about the arrival of the family in America and the fourth part profiles the life of each member of the Edwards family after they arrived in Philadelphia in the late 1840s. The profiles are arranged chronologically in the order in which the family members died.

The purpose of the narration is to document for posterity the sequence of major events in the life of the Edwards family; to bring them back to life, albeit only momentarily; and to depict their fundamental character and outlook on life as Scottish Lowland Presbyterian transplants to America.

The research for this family history was conducted in three general time frames. In the early 1950s, a family tree was compiled based on oral tradition in the Chambers family which stated that Annie (Edwards) Chambers, wife of George W. Chambers, was from Scotland and that she died when she was 82 years old.

About 1985, a letter was written to the National Archives in Washington, D.C., requesting a copy of George W. Chambers' Civil War pension file. The documents that were forthcoming from the National Archives included two brief sworn statements made in 1917 by Annie (Edwards) Chambers, widow of George W. Chambers. An examination of the documents revealed that (1) Annie (Edwards) Chambers' parents were Adam Edwards and Isabella Edwards; (2) her father died in 1850 and her mother died in 1863; (3) between 1858 to 1862 she resided with her mother and three brothers, George, William and Robert Edwards on Jones Street between 18th and 19th Streets in the 9th Ward of the City of Philadelphia; and (4) she was born on February 26, 1847, in Scotland. According to the sworn statement in the pension file, Annie (Edwards) Chambers, also produced the Edwards Family Bible published in Edinburgh, Scotland, in 1835, that contained an entry of her birth.

The balance of the original research was conducted between 1995 and 2000 in Washington, D.C., at the National Archives, the Library of Congress, the National Genealogical Society Library, and the Daughters of the American Revolution Library. Substantial research was also conducted at the Latter-Day Saints Family History Center located in McLean, Virginia. Site visits were made to the Free Library of Philadelphia, the Philadelphia City Archives, the Genealogical Society of Pennsylvania, and the Historical Society of Pennsylvania all located in Philadelphia and to Lawnview Cemetery located in Rockledge, Pennsylvania, as well as to the Pennsylvania Memorial located at the National Military Park in Gettysburg, Pennsylvania.

Interviews were conducted with two of the great-grandchildren of Annie (Edwards) Chambers both of whom descended from her oldest son, William Scott Chambers. Providing their recollections of their great-grandmother were the late William Scott Chambers and the late Josephine Thompson Marshall who were 6 ½-years-old and 11 ½-years-old, respectively, when their great-grandmother died.

Correspondence was carried out with several institutions and facilities including the Catholic Cemeteries Office in Philadelphia, Mount Moriah Cemetery, Forest Hills Cemetery, and the Pennsylvania Vital Statistics Office in New Castle as well as the Oliver Bair Funeral Home and the Garzone Funeral Home.

During the course of the original research, contact was reestablished with the descendants of Annie (Edwards) Chambers' youngest son, George E. Chambers, after a hiatus of over fifty years. Unfortunately, the descendants of her two married daughters, Lydia E. Smith Roe and Emma C. Spence, could not be located. No trace has been found of the Edwards Family Bible nor have any pictures been found of any members of the Edwards family.

Recently, an attempt was made to contact Edwards family descendants via public family trees posted to ancestry.com that included information about Annie (Edwards) Chambers' brother, William Scott Edwards, and her uncle, Alexander Edwards. The attempt was unsuccessful because the owners of the public family trees did not respond, were not directly related, or had no additional information.

Kathryn Chambers Torpey
February 14, 2016

Descendant Chart for Adam Edwards

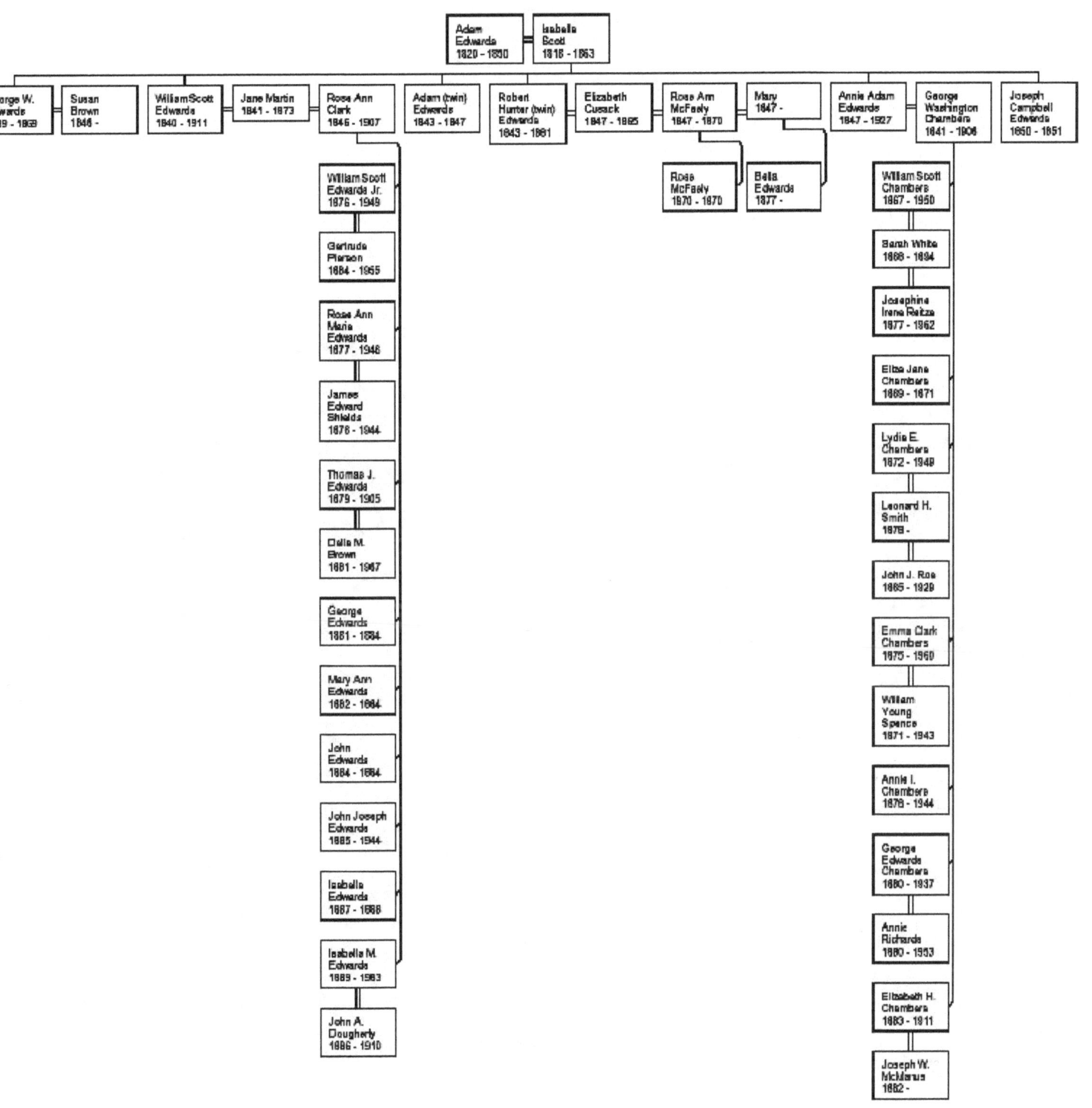

Adam Edwards 1820 – 1850 — **Isabella Scott** 1818 – 1863

- **George W. Edwards** 1839 – 1929
- **Susan Brown** 1846 –
- **William Scott Edwards** 1840 – 1911
- **Jane Martin** 1841 – 1873
- **Rose Ann Clark** 1846 – 1907
  - **William Scott Edwards Jr.** 1876 – 1949
  - **Gertrude Pierson** 1884 – 1965
  - **Rose Ann Marie Edwards** 1877 – 1948
  - **James Edward Shields** 1878 – 1944
  - **Thomas J. Edwards** 1879 – 1905
  - **Della M. Brown** 1881 – 1967
  - **George Edwards** 1881 – 1884
  - **Mary Ann Edwards** 1882 – 1884
  - **John Edwards** 1884 – 1884
  - **John Joseph Edwards** 1885 – 1944
  - **Isabella Edwards** 1887 – 1888
  - **Isabella M. Edwards** 1889 – 1983
  - **John A. Dougherty** 1886 – 1910
- **Adam (twin) Edwards** 1843 – 1847
- **Robert Hunter (twin) Edwards** 1843 – 1881
- **Elizabeth Cusack** 1847 – 1895
- **Rose Ann McFeely** 1847 – 1870
  - **Rose McFeely** 1870 – 1870
- **Mary** 1847 –
  - **Bella Edwards** 1877 –
- **Annie Adam Edwards** 1847 – 1927
- **George Washington Chambers** 1841 – 1906
  - **William Scott Chambers** 1867 – 1950
  - **Sarah White** 1868 – 1894
  - **Josephine Irene Reitze** 1877 – 1962
  - **Eliza Jane Chambers** 1869 – 1871
  - **Lydia E. Chambers** 1872 – 1949
  - **Leonard H. Smith** 1879 –
  - **John J. Roe** 1865 – 1929
  - **Emma Clark Chambers** 1875 – 1960
  - **William Young Spence** 1871 – 1943
  - **Annie I. Chambers** 1878 – 1944
  - **George Edwards Chambers** 1880 – 1937
  - **Annie Richards** 1880 – 1953
  - **Elizabeth H. Chambers** 1880 – 1911
  - **Joseph W. McManus** 1882 –
- **Joseph Campbell Edwards** 1850 – 1851

The Edwards/Scott Family History

Adam Edwards died unexpectedly on July 29, 1850.[1] Philadelphia was in the midst of a heat wave that week. Adam did not feel very well when he got up and left for work, but he had no idea that day was to be his last. Neither did his wife, Isabella, who was at home with their five young children, George, William, Robert, Annie, and Joseph.

Adam and Isabella Edwards had come to Philadelphia from Edinburgh, Scotland, a year earlier with their four oldest children. George was 9 when they left Edinburgh. William was 7, Robert was 4, and Annie was only 2 at the time of their crossing. They sailed in the company of Adam Edwards' oldest brother, Alexander, and his family.

Before they emigrated, they all lived in a flour milling settlement on the northern fringe of the Second New Town of Edinburgh, where Adam worked as a miller.[2] The family left home in hopes of a better life in America chiefly because opportunity was limited in Edinburgh after 1830. The Industrial Revolution had barely affected the city and its environs and much of the medieval Old Town had sunk into a moldering slum.[3]

Sadly, their hopes of a better life in America were not to be fulfilled. When Adam died and was laid to rest, Isabella was left destitute.

THE SCOTT FAMILY IN SCOTLAND

Adam Edwards' wife, Isabella, was the daughter of William Scott and Anne Brown. She was born on June 7, 1818, in Galashiels, County Selkirk, Scotland.[4] Her father was a farm servant and the family descended from Lowland Scottish Presbyterians who lived in the Borders.[5]

The Geography of the Borders and the Scottish Lowlands

Geographically, the Borders are in the southernmost part of the Scottish Lowlands. The Scottish Lowlands include that area from the narrow waist between Glasgow and Edinburgh and the coastal strip north of Edinburgh all the way south to the English border.[6] There are few natural barriers in the Scottish Lowlands to hinder the constant movement of people with the exception of some high hills and moors known as the Southern Uplands which rise in the interior part of the Lowlands to a height of more than 2,500 feet above sea level and several good sized rivers that flow through the region.

The Origins of the Scottish Lowlanders

Historically, Lowlander families of the 19th Century such as Isabella Scott's family descended from a mixture of many ancestral strains of people including the aboriginal people of the Stone Age, the Gaels (a Celtic people from the European continent who overran the entire island of Briton around 500 B.C.E.), the Teutonic Angles who dominated the eastern Lowland of Scotland for centuries, the Britons, the Saxons, the Romans, and the Scots (another Celtic tribe that invaded Scotland from Ireland), as well as Norse adventurers and pirates, the Normans and Flemish traders. In addition to all of these, Englishmen also came across the border to add to the mixture.[7]

The Mind and Character of the Scottish Lowlander

Lowlander families of the 19th Century typically descended from people who had survived many centuries of difficult living in a harsh environment. Their ancestors were a tough, stubborn people capable of enduring great hardship. This hardness of character was combined with a tendency toward violence in defense of what was theirs. They were also quick to take offense so as not to be considered weak.[8] Thus, Isabella's forebears in the Borders were not a submissive people as they spent much of their lives vigorously defending their homeland from the English. They also demanded independence of mind and the freedom to live their lives as they saw fit with no other telling them how to do so. In fact, it is said that they would not tolerate subservience of any kind except to the self-imposed authority of the Presbyterian Church.[9] This was the ancestral heritage of Isabella Scott.

County Selkirk (or Selkirkshire), Scotland

Isabella Scott traced part of her ancestral lineage to County Selkirk, an inland county of the Borders. In ancient times, County Selkirk was often referred to in royal charters as Ettrick Forest, a favorite hunting ground of the Scottish kings.[10] In fact, when Isabella Scott was a young girl, the remains of an ancient castle which was once the hunting lodge of the kings of Scotland and the home of the keeper of the forest was clearly visible on the banks of the Yarrow River. During the time Isabella Scott and her family lived in County Selkirk, the land was mainly in the possession of Melrose Abbey, the Duke of Buccleuch (to whom some of Isabella's ancestors pledged their allegiance), and various freeholders.[11,12]

County Selkirk is characterized by hills and valleys and four primary rivers - the Tweed, the Yarrow, the Ettrick, and the Gala. In the early part of the 19th Century, 10,000 acres in Selkirkshire were under cultivation, 2,300 acres were woodland, 1,250 acres were gardens and parklands, and the remainder was mountain pasture principally for sheep.[13]

Selkirk - The Chief County Town

The chief county town in County Selkirk was the royal burgh of Selkirk. From its proximity to the English border, Selkirk was the site in much earlier times of frequent invasions by the English that resulted in ferocious battles between England and Scotland for control of Briton.[14] It was also the town where Isabella Scott's parents, William Scott and Anne Brown were married on June 15, 1810.[15] And, it may be the town where William Scott and Anne Brown were baptized.[16,17]

After their marriage, William Scott and his wife, Anne Brown, appear to have moved six miles north to the market-town of Galashiels. It was there that they set up housekeeping. It was also in Galashiels that Isabella was born on June 7, 1818.[18] Isabella had at least two brothers, Andrew born on January 15, 1821, and William born on February 6, 1825.[19]

Galashiels is a very old town. At one time during the reign of David II (1329-1371), the Scottish Army was stationed in the immediate area and there are numerous accounts of battles and skirmishes having been waged against the English near Galashiels[20]. Nevertheless, by the time Isabella Scott was born, Galashiels had long since emerged from its early incarnation as little more than a settlement of huts (or shiels) by the banks of the Gala River where pilgrims stopped on their way north to pray at Melrose Abbey.[21] It had, in fact, become the most important market-town in County Selkirk. The market, held on Mondays, was well known and the fairs held on July 8 and October 8 were well attended.

Geographically, Galashiels comprised more than 10,000 acres of which about half were under cultivation. Five hundred acres were woodland or plantation, and the rest were pasture lands in the hills. The chief crops were oats, barley, wheat, potatoes, and turnips, and wool was beginning to emerge as an important product.[22] As early as 1790, 250 women were continuously employed spinning wool and looms numbered forty-three.[23]

The rivers Tweed, Ettrick, and Gala either skirted the town or ran directly through it. From time to time while Isabella was young, the Gala River would overflow its banks in a predictable pattern and threaten the town with inundation. Eventually, this dangerous situation was remedied, but as late as 1829, the town was almost completely destroyed by a flood except that some residents had the presence of mind to chop down an entire stand of trees on the banks of the Gala River and throw them into the river to divert the torrential flow away from the town.[24] Isabella had left Galashiels for Edinburgh long before 1843 when it became a small, straggling industrial town that later emerged as the premier tweed producing town in Scotland.[25]

County Roxburgh (or Roxburghshire), Scotland

Another part of Isabella Scott's ancestral lineage can be traced to Ashkirk, Minto, and possibly Hawick in County Roxburgh which is southeast of County Selkirk and abuts the border with England. This area of Scotland is deep in that part of the Borders originally controlled by the Scotts. The main road, which runs from Hawick to Selkirk, cuts through the interior of County Roxburgh. The village and parish of Ashkirk stands on the main road. In earlier times, all of the land in the parish of Ashkirk was wholly divided among the Scotts.[26] The villages of Minto and Lilliesleaf are nearby as is the largest of the Borders towns, Hawick, which was granted by the Scottish crown to the Scotts of Buccleuch in the early 16th Century. Hawick suffered great devastation during the invasions of 1544, 1545, and 1547 when the English tried unsuccessfully to impose union by force.[27]

THE EDWARDS FAMILY IN SCOTLAND

Adam Edwards was born in Edinburgh on October 22, 1820. His parents were George Edwards and Agnes Adam.[28] Although Edwards is not a Scottish surname, it can be traced to Edinburgh as early at the 15th Century.

Edinburgh, Midlothian (or Edinburghshire), Scotland

Edinburgh, which is in the Scottish Lowlands, was built on a series of hills that rise from a level plain about two miles south of the Firth of Forth. The plain is only about 94 feet above sea level. It is upon this plain that the Palace of Holyroodhouse has stood since 1503 when it was officially established as the royal residence of the Scottish Kings by James IV. From this plain, a central hill rises in the form of a flat ridge upon which the Old Town of Edinburgh was built in about 1140. The ridge terminates in a precipitous rock on whose summit Edinburgh Castle was built in the 7th Century at a height of 274 feet above sea level.

St. Cuthbert's Parish and Church

The Church of Scotland is Presbyterian.[29] The Presbyterian Church was established as the national church in 1690. The Edwards family is known to have lived in St. Cuthbert's Civil Parish (also known as West Church Parish). Some of their family marriages and baptisms were recorded in the registers of St. Cuthbert's Kirk located immediately beside Edinburgh Castle.

The Kirk was built on an 8th Century Culdee foundation dedicated to St. Cuthbert of the Lothians (c. 635-687).[30] The Kirk is first mentioned by name in the Holyrood Charter dated about 1140. Being so close to Edinburgh Castle, the Kirk suffered a great deal of damage over the years when it was used repeatedly as a battery during at least four sieges of Edinburgh in 1573, 1640, 1650, and, lastly, in 1689 when Edinburgh Castle was attacked by William of Orange.

EDWARDS FAMILY MARRIAGES. As a consequence of all this warfare, the Kirk was rebuilt many time. The church which still stands today beside Edinburgh Castle is of a basilica-type construction. When it was erected in 1892, the foundations of at least six earlier churches were found. Its immediate predecessor is described as a plain, box-like building constructed in 1775 to which a steeple was added in 1789.[31]

It was in this earlier church that the following Edwards family events took place:

> George Edwards to Agnes Adam daughter of John Adam on May 17, 1806 (BANNS ONLY)[32]
> Alexander Edwards to Margaret McIntosh daughter of Peter McIntosh on April 6, 1835[33]
> Adam Edwards to Isabella Scott daughter of Willaim Scott on December 28, 1838[34]

EDWARDS FAMILY BAPTISMS. All six of the children known to have been born to George Edwards, miller at Gorgie Mills, and his wife, Agnes Adam, daughter of John Adam who resided at Dundee, were baptized in St. Cuthbert's Kirk. The children's names were recorded in the Kirk baptismal registers as follows:

> Alexander born on June 19, 1810, baptized July 10, 1810
> Robert born on July 18, 1812, baptized August 10, 1812,
> George born on October 15, 1815, baptized November 8, 1815
> Susan born on September 19, 1818, baptized October 3, 1818
> Adam born on October 22, 1820
> Jane born on September 1, 1825[35]

Only one of the five children known to have been born to Adam Edwards and Isabella Scott while they lived in Edinburgh appears to have been recorded in the St. Cuthbert's Kirk registers. His name was recorded in the Kirk baptismal register as George born September 24, 1839.[36]

Only two of the four children known to have been born to Alexander Edwards and Margaret McIntosh while they lived in Edinburgh appear to have been recorded in the St. Cuthbert's Kirk registers. Their names were recorded in the Kirk baptismal register as Ann born May 9, 1837 and George born February 21, 1840.[37]

Why the baptisms of the remaining children of Adam Edwards or those of his oldest brother, Alexander Edwards, were not recorded in the St. Cuthbert's Kirk baptismal registers is unknown. The registers may no longer exist or the children may have been baptized at another church.[38] Or the families may have joined the Free Church of Scotland established in 1843.[39] Or the United Presbyterian Church established in Scotland in 1847.[40]

Notwithstanding this lack of information concerning the specific Presbyterian Church that the Edwards family may have attended in Edinburgh after 1840, Annie Adam (Edwards) Chambers, asserted in a deposition she gave on June 3, 1910, in Philadelphia that:

> My parents were Presbyterians and the children were all baptized and christened
> in the Presbyterian Church when infants. [However], I do not know in what
> church in Edinboro (sic) they were christened.[41]

The News Towns of Edinburgh

Even though the Edwards family marriages and baptisms were recorded in the registers of St. Cuthbert's Kirk in the Old Town of Edinburgh from 1806 until at least 1840, they did not live in the Old Town.[42] Instead, the records at St. Cuthbert's Kirk clearly state that from 1806 until at least 1825, George Edwards, his wife, Agnes Adam, and their children actually lived in Gorgie Mills, a small village situated about two miles west of the Old Town of Edinburgh on the road to Glasgow. Gorgie Mills is traceable to 1636. It was then part of Gorgie, a scattered agricultural and milling community to the west of the Old Town of Edinburgh. The name Gorgie is said to derive from the Old Welsh *gorgyne* meaning a spacious wedge of land between Craiglockhart Hills and the Leith River at Saughton.

In 1835, the marriage register at St. Cuthbert's Kirk states that their oldest son, Alexander Edward, and his future wife, Margaret McIntosh, were both residing in Canonmills. Canonmills was about 2.3 miles from Gorgie Mills. It was part of the Second New Town of Edinburgh which was laid out in 1802 on the steep slope of the Leith River directly to the north of the First New Town. The First New Town lies north of the Old Town and was begun in 1767 with the draining of North Loch and the building of North Bridge. After the formation of the First New Town, extensive additions were made to the city in all directions.[43]

In 1838, their youngest son, Adam Edwards, was stated in the marriage register of St. Cuthbert's Kirk to be living at # 3 Warriston Street (sic) located immediately across the Leith River from Canonmills.[44,45] His future wife, Isabella Scott, was stated to be living on Canon Street in Canonmills.

In 1841, the census of Scotland enumerates Adam Edwards, his wife, Isabella, and their son, George, at No. 3 Canon Street and his oldest brother, Alexander Edwards, his wife, Margaret, and their son, George, at No. 6 Canon Street.[46,47] These addresses were on the same street in Canonmills in the Second New Town of Edinburgh.

Canonmills - The Flour-Milling Settlement

Canonmills was an ancient milling settlement that grew up beside Stockbridge on the right bank of the Leith River about a mile away from Edinburgh Castle. As far back as the 12th Century, the Baxters' (or Bakers') Incorporation of Edinburgh was obligated by law to grind their corn at Canonmills which was then worked by the Augustinian canons of Holyrood Abbey.

Canonmills was originally a small suburb of Edinburgh, but it was later incorporated into the northern outskirts of the Second New Town.[48] Exactly what Canonmills may have been like when the Adam Edwards and his oldest brother, Alexander, lived there with their families is unknown, but about 1861 it was described as a mean, plebeian, confused little suburb.[49]

Employment, Trade and Manufacturing

Unfortunately, the scale of the 19th Century Industrial Revolution barely affected Edinburgh in comparison to other Scottish cities such as Glasgow and Dundee.

It is, therefore, not surprising that the registers of St. Cuthbert's Kirk indicate that George Edwards and both his sons, Alexander and Adam, worked as millers. At that time, the traditional industries of Edinburgh were printing and publishing, flour milling and biscuit-baking, and brewing. There was also a small, but important ship building industry in Edinburgh. Nevertheless, much of the industry of the city, such as furniture, ironworks, pottery and glass, was conducted on a small scale in workshops of skilled craftsmen.[50]

Married Life in Edinburgh

On June 3, 1910, a Special Examiner of the Bureau of Pensions took a deposition from Annie Adam (Edwards) Chambers, the only daughter of Adam Edwards and Isabella Scott, concerning her brother, William Scott Edwards' claim for an increase in his Civil War pension.[51] During the course of her deposition, Annie Adam (Edwards) Chambers was asked by the examiner to tell the early history of her family in Scotland as she knew it. The following account is extracted from her deposition.

> My parents married young, father 17 and mother 18 years old at the time.[52]
>
> Their first child was George not William Scott; then Robert and Adam, twins; then myself; and then the little one born here, Joseph Campbell.
>
> My parents lived in Edinboro (sic) and all the children except the youngest was born in Edinboro (sic). My parents were Presbyterians and the children were all baptized and christened in the Presbyterian Church when infants. I do not know in what church in Edinboro (sic) they were christened. I was not quite 16 years old when my mother died and all I know about the family history is what I used to hear mother tell. I have always had a good memory and can remember a good deal my mother told me.
>
> Mother married in 1838. I have here in my possession mother's original marriage certificate.[53] [Hands examiner said certificate. It is very old, creased and torn, and the ink is very faded. It is undoubtedly genuine. It reads as follows:
>
>> At St. Cuthbert's (Cuthbert's) the twenty fourth day of December 1838. It is hereby certified that Adam Edward, Miller, Residing in No. 3 Warriston Crescent (sic), Parish of St. Cuthbert's and Isabella Scott, Residing in Canon Street Canonmills, Same Parish, Daughter of William Scott, Farm Servant in Peebles, have been three times duly and regularly proclaimed in order to Marriage in the Parish Church of St. Cuthberts and no objection offered.[54]
>>
>> A.W. McFullanton, Elder
>> John Adams, Session Clerk
>
> Amount of Fee, 10s 6d
>
>> At Edinburgh the 28th day of December, 1838, that Adam Edward and Isabella Scott were this day married by me is here certified.
>>
>> James McFarland, Minister]
>
> George was born first, some time in 1839. I can't remember for certain the

month, but I think it was November 1839.[55] He was born before they had been married a year anyway.

William was the next child and was born August 17th 1840. I am not certain as to the year, but I am as to the day of the month. I have always remembered the month and day of the month that William was born. I often heard my mother mention it. I also distinctly remember hearing mother say that her first two children came very quick and that her parents scolded her for having children so fast.

I feel certain that George was born in 1839 and about November; and William in August of the next year. 1840. It couldn't have been 1841 as I know mother always said he came pretty soon after George. The twins were born in September 1843; and I was born February 26, 1847.

It seems to me that mother did have a little small Bible with our births in it, but I have no idea about [what]ever became of it. I think I had it after my mother's death, but lost all track of that Bible years ago.

The Edwards Family Bible

On February 15, 1917, Annie Adam (Edwards) Chambers appeared before a Notary Public for the Commonwealth of Pennsylvania to give a statement in connection with her claim for an increase in her Civil War widow's pension.[56] The following information about the Edwards Family Bible is extracted from her statement.

The deponent, [Annie Adam (Edwards) Chambers], says that she was born on the 26th day of February 1847 in Scotland and she has this day produced before me a Family Bible in which the births and deaths of the family are recorded, the Bible having been published in Edinburg, (sic) Scotland and bears date 1835. The record of the birth of Ann Edwards shows as February 26th, 1847, a figure 6 has been written over the figure 7, but the original entry 1847 can be distinguished. The condition of the bible is such as to look as if used in the years corresponding with the dates of the births and deaths and the records of the births and deaths look original. The deponent further declares that the record of the birth of Ann Edwards is the record of her birth, but that she has always been known and called by the name Annie and not Ann, and that her maiden name was Annie Edwards.[57]

THE EDWARDS FAMILY'S ARRIVAL IN AMERICA

Adam Edwards and his family along with his oldest brother, Alexander Edwards, and his family arrived at the Port of New York on July 30, 1849, aboard the Bark Mary.[58]

The master of the Bark Mary was Captain Nathan Moses. The vessel was a British-owned 237.5 ton, three-masted sailing ship built of wood.[59] The ship was reported in the New York Herald to have departed the Port of Glasgow loaded with iron and 165 passengers. According to the notice of arrival, the crossing took 41 days which was a long voyage even in those days and, possibly, an indication of foul weather and/or some other type of unfavorable sailing conditions.

The official passenger manifest for the Bark Mary shows that the first eleven people to board the ship were the following members of the Edwards family:

Alex Edwards	38 years
Margaret do	38 years
George do	9 years
Peter do	6 years
Robert do	4 years
Allen (sic) do	29 years
Isabella do	31 years
George do	9 years
William do	7 years
Robert do	4 years
Anne do	Infant[60]

There were no cabin passengers listed on the manifest so everyone, including the Edwards family, was probably crammed into steerage. For some unexplained reason, all passengers on the Bark Mary including all the women, children, and infants were listed as German laborers. Judging from the passengers' surnames as listed on the ship's manifest, however, this entry concerning their country of origin was probably incorrect.

Notwithstanding this oddity in the passenger list entry and the misspelling in Adam Edwards' first name, there can be little doubt that this is the correct Edwards family. This conclusion is further supported by a deposition given by Annie Adam (Edwards) Chambers, on June 3, 1910, in which she said:

> With my parents came four children to this country. They are all dead [now], but William and me. ... My father died in Philadelphia in 1850 a year after he came to this country.[61]

THE EDWARDS FAMILY IN AMERICA

Adam Edwards and his family seem to have taken up residence in Philadelphia shortly after their arrival in America and lived there all the rest of their lives.

Adam Edwards - Father

Adam Edwards died unexpectedly during a week of extremely hot weather in Philadelphia. In the local news section of *The Dollar Newspaper*, a weekly published in Philadelphia on August 7, 1850, eight people were reported to have died the week of July 28, 1850, from the excessive heat of the day; exposure to the sun; sun stroke; effects of sun stroke; effects of the heat; a stroke of the sun; being struck by the sun; and the effects of extreme heat.[62]

The report filed by Doctor G. Watson stated that Adam Edwards died of Congestion of the Brain from the Heat.[63,64] Although Doctor Watson dated the death report July 30, 1850, he did not actually indicate the date that Adam Edwards died.

Adam Edwards' obituary which appeared in the *Philadelphia Public Ledger* on Wednesday, July 31, 1850, documents his date of death as follows:

> Suddenly, on the 29th inst., ADAM EDWARDS, late of Edinburgh, Scotland, in the 29th year of his age.
>
> The friends and acquaintances of the family are respectfully invited to attend the funeral from his late residence, in Carlton street, above Thirteenth, this (Wednesday) Afternoon at 4 o'clock.[65]

The only other clue that has been uncovered concerning Adam Edwards' death is contained in a deposition given by his son, William Scott Edwards, on June 1, 1910, concerning his request for an increase in his Civil War pension. In that deposition, William Scott Edwards also states that his father died July 29, 1850.[66]

The Odd Fellows Cemetery Register of Interments states that Adam Edwards, miller, was buried on July 31, 1850.[67] This is consistent with the burial date contained in the cemetery returns filed for the week ending August 3, 1850, indicating that Adam Edwards was buried in the Odd Fellows Cemetery located at 23rd and Diamond Streets.[68] It is possible that he may have belonged to the Independent Order of Odd Fellows (IOOF) except that the Register of Interments indicates he was buried in the Strangers' Ground, Lot 413, Block 5, Grave 22 West. If he did belong to the IOOF, his widow, Isabella, and the children may have received financial assistance from them after he died.

Exactly where Adam Edwards lived at the time of his death is confusing. He was reported in the mortality schedule to have died in July after having been sick for 3 days due to having become overheated on the job where he worked as a laborer.[69] On August 13, 1850, *his widow, Isabella*, was reported to be living in Spring Garden Ward 4 with her five children - George, William, Robert, Annie, and Joseph.[70] And, his brother, Alexander Edwards, was reported to be living nearby in Spring Garden Ward 4 with his wife, Margaret, and their four children - George, Peter, Robert and Margaret.[71] Then, on September 3, 1850, *the late Adam Edwards* was enumerated with his family in North Mulberry Ward which was then located immediately below Vine Street a very short distance from Spring Garden Ward 4.[72] Since the official date for the 1850 census was June 1, 1850, the late Adam Edwards was correctly reported to be living with his family in the second enumeration because he did not die until July 29, 1850.

The name of the church from which Adam Edwards was buried is unknown although it was most likely a Presbyterian church in the neighborhood. There is no evidence that he left a will or that he owned any property. Assuming he died intestate, there is no record that his wife (or anyone else) filed a petition for Letters of Administration to settle his estate.

Little else is known about Adam Edwards' short life in America except that on September 13, 1951, (101 years after he was buried in the Odd Fellows Cemetery) he was removed to Lawnview Cemetery in Rockledge, Montgomery County, Pennsylvania, where he still rests today, alone, in an unmarked grave, in the Susquehanna Lawn Section of the cemetery.[73]

Joseph Campbell Edwards - The Youngest Son

The baby died next of enteritis. He was only 9 months old when he expired and was laid to rest in Ronaldson's Cemetery located at 10th and Wharton Streets.[74,75] He was buried in a plot belonging to the Scots Thistle Society.[76] No obituary was found in the *Philadelphia Public Ledger*, but his death record reads:

> Died January 11th 1851 of Enteritis, Joseph Campbell infant son of Adam Edwards, aged 9 months.[77]
>
> Colin Arrott, M.D.[78]

Nothing more is known about the baby other than the information about him that is contained in Annie Adam (Edwards) Chambers' deposition to the effect that:

> He was a little boy born in Philadelphia and died six months after father died. ...
> Their first child was George not William Scott, then Robert and Adam, twins,
> then myself; and then the little one born here, Joseph Campbell.[79]

At some point, 13,500 bodies were removed from Ronaldson's Cemetery to Forest Hills Cemetery located at 101 Byberry Road just inside the city limits of Philadelphia.[80] Joseph Campbell Edwards was one of those removals. He is buried there today in a mass grave.[81]

Isabella (Scott) Edwards Flanagan - Mother

Very little is known about life in the Edwards household after Adam and the baby died.

Every day was undoubtedly a difficult struggle for Isabella as she had four very young children to raise and no particular skills. Indeed, the decade of the 1850s was one of great hardship for many people in Philadelphia. Work was frequently unavailable. Wages were low. Epidemics were common. Medical care was uneven. Summers were hot and winters were harsh. Nevertheless, true to their Scottish heritage, Isabella and her children persevered.

According to the 1852 Philadelphia City Directory, Isabella Edwards resided at Carlton Street above Schuylkill 6th (now 17th Street).[82] This address is about three blocks west of Carlton Street, above 13th, the family's residence at the time of Adam Edwards' death in 1850.

There is no information in the 1852 City Directory about Isabella Edwards' occupation nor are there any further listings for Isabella Edwards after 1852. From that time forward, the family's movements can only be ascertained from a sworn statement given by Annie Adam

(Edwards) Chambers (Isabella's daughter) on March 19, 1917, in which she states the following about where the family lived:

> The deponent [Annie Adam (Edwards) Chambers] further states that she resided with her mother and three brothers George, William and Robert Edwards on Jones Street between 18th and 19th Streets, in the 9th Ward of the City of Philadelphia, between the years 1858 to 1862; [and after that the] deponent resided at # 3 Curry's Court, which ran off Jones Street between 19th and 20th Streets and Market and Filbert Streets, in the said Ward and City, between the years 1862 and 1864...[83]

MARRIAGE TO ANDREW FLANAGAN. It is apparent, based on the following evidence, that sometime between 1852 and 1860, Isabella (Scott) Edwards married a man named Andrew Flanagan who worked as a laborer and as a boatman.[84,85,86]

Interestingly, their mother's remarriage is never mentioned by either Annie Adam (Edwards) Chambers or her brother, William Scott Edwards, in any of the various depositions and sworn statements they each gave in support of increases in their Civil War pensions

That she remarried at least once is indisputable. Absent a corroborating entry in a marriage register, the evidence of her remarriage is as follows:

First, all of the family (except George Edwards) is enumerated in the 1860 census schedule, on June 26, 1860, living together, in the 9th Ward of the city, north of Market Street as follows:

Andrew Flanagan	[3]0 years old	male	Boatman	born in Ireland
Isabella "	35 years old	female		born in Scotland
W.E. (sic) Edwards	17 years old	male	Porter Bottler	born in Scotland
Rob. "	12 years old	male		born in Scotland
Fanny (sic) "	11 years old	female		born in Scotland[87]

It appears from this census schedule entry that Isabella (Scott) Edwards was being enumerated as the wife of Andrew Flanagan. The census schedule also shows that the Flanagan/Edwards family was sharing a house with the families of Alexander Kelly and George Proctor.[88] Later, in 1864, it appears that this same Alexander Kelly was a witness for William Scott Edwards when he was naturalized.

Second, Andrew Flanagan is known to have lived at the National Soldiers Home - Central Branch in Dayton, Montgomery County, Ohio from late in 1880 until his death in 1882. This home was one of several established by the Federal government after the Civil War for the relief of disabled officers and men of the volunteer forces of the United States.[89] In the Register of the Soldiers Home in Dayton, Ohio, there is a notation in the records of Andrew Flanagan that his step-children were named William Edwards and Annie Chambers.[90]

THE DEATH OF ISABELLA (SCOTT) EDWARDS FLANAGAN. William Scott Edwards states in a deposition he gave on June 1, 1910, that he recalled his mother dying on July 13 (sic), 1863.[91] His recollection appears to be in error given the following obituary for her that appeared on July 28, 1863:

> FLANIGAN (sic) - On the 25th inst., Isabella, wife of Andrew Flanigan (sic), aged 45 years.
>
> The relatives and friends of the family are respectfully invited to attend the funeral from her husband's residence, No. 3 Washington Court, Jones Street, west of Nineteenth, this (Tuesday) afternoon at 1o'clock - to proceed to Mount Moriah Cemetery.[92]

THE BURIAL OF ISABELLA (SCOTT) EDWARDS FLANAGAN. The 1863 Death Register for the City of Philadelphia states that Isabella Flannigan (sic) died of dysentery on July 25, 1863.[93] In the death register she is described as a 46-year-old married woman who was born in Scotland. Her address is listed as Johns (sic) Street and 18th in the 9th Ward of the city.

She was buried at Mount Moriah Cemetery on July 28, 1863 in Section 108, Lot 010 SE-1/4.[94] The plot is said to have belonged to a man named William Rountree.[95] Buried with Isabella (Scott) Edwards Flanagan are at least eight other people including her son, George Edwards, and her daughter-in-law, Lizzie Edwards, the wife of her son, Robert Edwards.[96] The relationship, if any, of Isabella (Scott) Edwards Flanagan to the others buried in this plot is unknown. A visit to Mount Moriah Cemetery revealed that there are no headstones on this plot.[97]

THE LIFE AND TIMES OF ANDREW FLANAGAN. According to Andrew Flanagan's military service record, he was mustered in as a Private in Company G of the 66th Regiment of the Pennsylvania Volunteer Infantry on August 9, 1861, for a three year term.[98] On March 1, 1862, he was transferred to Company K of the 99th Regiment of the Pennsylvania Volunteer Infantry where he served out the rest of his enlistment.

He was described in a Furlough contained in his military service record as 34 years old in May 1864. This would have made him approximately 12 years younger than his late wife, Isabella. He was also described as 5 feet, 5-1/2 inches tall, of light complexion, blue eyes, and light hair. He was born in Ireland.[99] His occupation prior to enlistment was recorded as a boatman.

Among the many battles in which Andrew Flanagan participated during the Civil War was the Battle of Gettysburg. According to Taylor's *Philadelphia in the Civil War*,

> The 99th, under the command of Major John W. Moore, made the forced march to the field of Gettysburg from Emmitsburg, making its bivouac on the night of July 1st in the Peach Orchard. In the formation of the troops in front of Little Round Top on the 2nd, the position of the 99th was near Devils' Den. Here the 99th defended its position gallantly until relieved by a division of the Fifth Army Corps, then pushing forward, in support of Webb's Brigade of the Second Corp, to the Emmitsburg Pike, where it remained until the morning of July 4th. The

official report indicates that the 99th reached Gettysburg with three hundred and thirty-nine officers and men, losing in killed, wounded and missing one hundred and ten.[100]

Thus, Andrew Flanagan was not present in Philadelphia on July 25, 1863, when his wife, Isabella, died and it is doubtful that she ever knew whether he survived the Battle of Gettysburg.

Andrew Flanagan was mustered out of the service on September 6, 1864, by reason of expiration of his time of enlistment. According to his service record:

> The bounty of $100 is due the soldier. He participated in all the Battles up to the Battle of the Wilderness where he was wounded and has been absent since in Hospital at Philadelphia. May 5/64

He may actually have spent some time in the Soldiers Home in the City of Philadelphia. This facility was incorporated on April 9, 1864, as the first institution of its kind established in the United States.[101] Their records show an entry for an Andrew Falligan (sic) who was admitted briefly to the home on May 20, 1867 and was later discharged as "improved."[102] Thereafter, he appears to have resumed living with the Edwards children as he was listed repeatedly in the city directories as follows:

1867	Flanagan, Edward (sic)	boatman, r 1725 Moravian Street
1867/8	Flannigan (sic), Andrew	boatman, h 1725 Moravian Street
1868/9	Flannery (sic), Andrew	boatman, h 1725 Moravian Street
1869	Flanagan, Andrew	boatman, h r 1725 Moravian Street

Although he has not been found in the first enumeration of the 1870 census, he was listed in the second enumeration at the rear of 1725 Moravian Street with his step-son, William Scott Edwards, and William's first wife, Jane (Martin) Edwards.[103]

Andrew Flanagan appears to have submitted an original Civil War invalid pension application on December 5, 1874, while he was living at 1725 Moravian Street. What happened to him between 1874 and 1880 is unclear. Apparently, his request for a pension was not processed at that time and there are no obvious listings for him in the Philadelphia city directories (except for a possible listing in 1877 at 4639 Westminster Avenue).

He was not listed in the 1880 census at the National Soldiers Home in Dayton, Ohio.[104] Nevertheless, he appears to have been admitted to that home shortly after the census was taken as the Register at the Soldiers Home indicates that his date of admission was [----] 24, 1880.[105] He later swore to an affidavit on July 12, 1881, in Dayton, Ohio, in connection with his pension application which was approved, subsequently, on April 6, 1882.[106] At the time his pension was approved, he was declared to be one-quarter disabled due to a gun shot wound to his left leg which he sustained at the Battle of the Wilderness. He was awarded a pension of $2.00 per month payable quarterly retroactive to September 7, 1864.[107]

THE DEATH OF ANDREW FLANAGAN. Andrew Flanagan died of apoplexy (i.e., paralysis due to stroke) on May 12, 1882, (a little over one month after his pension was approved) while on furlough in Philadelphia from the National Soldiers Home in Dayton, Ohio.[108] He was buried on May 15, 1882, by the Anna M. Ross Post, No. 94, Grand Army of the Republic (GAR), in the Soldiers Home Plot at Mount Moriah Cemetery (Section 133, Lot 115).[109,110,111] The Soldiers Home Plot was donated to the Soldiers Home in the City of Philadelphia on May 17, 1863, by Robert P. King, president of the Mount Moriah Cemetery Association.[112]

On October 23, 1883, the Soldiers Monument was dedicated at Mount Moriah Cemetery upon the lot in which Andrew Flanagan was buried which contains the graves of sixty soldiers.[113] The inscription on the monument reads as follows:

> Erected by the Soldiers Home of the City of Philadelphia
>
> To the honored memory of the brave who defended their country's rights in the perils of the great conflict between North and South.

After he died, William Scott Edwards and Annie Adam (Edwards) Chambers applied to the National Soldiers Home in Dayton for his effects. The official record reads that:

> The application of Wm Edwards and Annie Chambers (step-children of Andrew Flanagan deceased) for the Effects of Flannagan (sic) was denied by the Board of Managers at their meeting on July 11, 1882. The application of Wm H. Drum - attorney for Wm Edwards and Annie Chambers - step-children of Andrew Flannigan (sic), was approved by the Board Managers - at their meeting in April 1883 - and vouchers of $229.14 in their favor were sent to the Treasurer's Office on May 12, 1883."[114]

Although no obituary appeared in the Philadelphia newspapers to commemorate his passing, Annie Adam (Edwards) Chambers and William Scott Edwards probably mourned the loss of their step-father. He was the only father they really ever knew and he undoubtedly rescued them and their mother, Isabella (Scott) Edwards, from what were unquestionably dire circumstances following the untimely death of Adam Edwards.

George Edwards - The Oldest Son

Exactly why George Edwards was not enumerated with his mother, Isabella (Scott) Edwards Flanagan and the rest of the Edwards family in the 1860 census is unknown at this time. It may have been an oversight as he does not appear in the census index under his own name.

BECOMING A CITIZEN. George Edwards was naturalized on October 25, 1860, one month after his twenty-first birthday, in the Court of Common Pleas for the City and County of Philadelphia.[115] His witness was George Leacock.[116]

WORK HISTORY. There is no evidence that George Edwards ever served in the Civil War. In city directories published subsequent to 1860, his occupation appears to be listed as follows:

1862   laborer, 1820 Jones Street
1864   laborer, rear of 1907 Jones Street
1865   driver, 1155 S 16th Street *(uncertain)*
1866   expressman, 1137 S 16th Street *(uncertain)*
1869   driver, h 2113 Carlton

SPRING GARDEN ENGINE COMPANY. In addition to working as a laborer or as a driver, George Edwards appears to have been a member of Spring Garden Engine Company No. 43.[117] Unfortunately, no record exists of his service with this organization because the records were badly kept at that time.[118] Nevertheless, according to the records maintained by the Fireman's Hall, this fire company is believed to have been disbanded on March 7, 1848, by the courts, but formed again on December 11, 1852. It is thought to have been located at 1903 Callowhill Street. Its motto was "Ever Ready to Assist the Needy."

The volunteer firemen were a huge power in Philadelphia. The volunteer fire companies were usually composed of neighbors and the social status of the companies depended upon where they were located in the city. That is, all the members of the fire companies were said to be honest men and good citizens, but some of them were more wealthy and more powerful than others.[119] This invariably led to strong competition among the companies in battling fires as well as to constant disorder and breaches of the peace. The volunteers were, in fact, quite rowdy. In later years, they became violent. Eventually, these problems became so great that a paid department was organized and placed in operation on March 3, 1871 and all the volunteer companies in the city were disbanded.[120]

MARRIAGE TO SUSAN BROWN. George Edwards married Susan Brown on August 27, 1865, at the Church of the Redemption, a Protestant Episcopal church located at 400 N. 22nd Street.[121,122] The Reverend George A. Durborrow officiated at the ceremony. At the time of their marriage, George was 24 and Susan Brown was 19. He was working as a bottler.

MEMBERSHIP IN SECRET SOCIETIES. George Edwards also appears to have belonged to at least two secret societies - the Knights of Pythias and the American Protestant Association.[123] The Knights of Pythias was a secret and beneficial society established in Washington, D.C., on February 19, 1864. It included endowment sections that paid death benefits to widows and orphans and uniform divisions in which members participated in military drills. The first lodge was organized in Philadelphia on February 19, 1867. Between then and September 9, 1867, eleven lodges were formed in Philadelphia including Liberty Lodge No. 11 to which George Edwards belonged. By 1884, there were 95 lodges in Philadelphia with twelve thousand members.[124]

The American Protestant Association (APA) was organized in Pittsburgh sometime between 1840 and 1850. It was an anti-Roman Catholic secret society with rituals and degrees whose emphasis was maintaining civil and religious liberties and the Bible in the public schools. Although it admitted Protestant citizens of foreign birth, it somehow became associated with the

Know Nothing Party campaigns of nativism that swept certain segments of the country between 1850 and 1856. At its highest point, its membership numbered more than 200,000.[125]

THE DEATH OF GEORGE EDWARDS. George Edwards died of heart disease on March 11, 1869. His obituary appeared in the *Philadelphia Public Ledger* as follows:

> EDWARDS, Suddenly on the 11th instant, George Edwards, in the 30th year of his age.
>
> The relatives and friends of the family; also Joshua Lodge No. 14 A.P.A. and Liberty Lodge No. 11 K. of P. and the Spring Garden Engine Company No. 43 are respectfully invited to attend the funeral from his late residence 2133 Carlton Street on Sunday afternoon at 1 o'clock without further notice. To proceed to Mount Moriah Cemetery.[126]

Based on his obituary, George Edwards appears to have lived a fairly active life for a man with heart disease. After he died, he was buried at Mount Moriah Cemetery in the same plot as his mother.[127] The plot is said to have belonged to a man named William Rountree.[128]

DYING INTESTATE. On March 23, 1869, George Edwards' widow, Susan (Brown) Edwards, filed a petition with the Register of Wills swearing that George Edwards died without a will.[129] She also stated in her petition that his estate did not exceed $500.00 and that she wished to be appointed Administratrix. She, along with James Roundtree and Samuel Liggett, posted the required bond after which she was granted Letters of Administration to settle the estate. Her address at the time was listed as the N.W. corner of 16th & Becket, below Coates.

Nothing more is known of the fate of Susan (Brown) Edwards except that she seems to have been enumerated in the 1870 census living in the 15th Ward of the city with the family of William Cook. She was at that time working as a dressmaker.[130,131]

Robert Edwards - The Surviving Twin

Robert Edwards is a shadowy figure. Although he always seems to be present, his essential self is hard to capture. According to a deposition given by his sister, Annie Adam (Edwards) Chambers, on June 3, 1910, Robert Edwards was one of a set of twins whose baby brother, Adam, died in Scotland when the twins were only about four years old.[132]

Robert Edwards was enumerated in the 1860 census schedule along with his step-father, Andrew Flanagan, his mother, Isabella (Scott) Edwards Flanagan and the rest of the family (except his brother, George) while the family was living at 1820 Jones Street.[133] In this census schedule, Robert's age was misreported as 12 instead of 17 and no occupation was listed.[134]

SERVICE IN THE CIVIL WAR. During the Civil War, Robert Edwards enlisted as a Private in Company C of the 109th Regiment (also known as the Curtain Light Guards) of the Pennsylvania Volunteer Infantry. He enlisted in Philadelphia on March 3, 1862, for a period of three years.[135] His age was recorded as 19. He was described as 5 feet, 8-1/2 inches tall, of fair complexion, blue eyes, and brown hair. His place of birth was recorded as Scotland.

According to Robert Edwards' compiled military service record for the 109th Regiment, he was present with his Regiment at the Battle of Cedar Mountain on August 9, 1862, where General Stonewall Jackson, with superior numbers, struck the Union forces. Although the hard-fought engagement was indecisive, many Union soldiers were lost. The 109th Regiment entered the battle with about three hundred and fifty, rank and file, and of those nearly one-half were either killed captured, or wounded. According to an eye-witness account:

> The brigades of Generals (sic) Geary and General Prince [of Banks Corp.]
> fought with the most desperate courage.[136] There was no running, shirking, or
> skulking whatsoever. I saw them as they went into the battle, and saw their
> ranks, thinned and bleeding, return. Truly has the spot where lie so many dead
> and wounded been called Slaughter Mountain.[137]

Twenty days later, during the Battles of Bull Run (Second Manassas), the 109th Regiment was committed again to the care of Banks' Corps, Army of Northern Virginia, where they were assigned to guard trains and destroy any of the Union stores that could not be gotten away safely. Thus, according to the official record of troop movements for Company C to which Robert Edwards was assigned:

> ... the whole of the company's knapsacks containing clothing, blankets,
> overcoats & likewise company property were abandoned & brunt for want of
> transportation on the march in the vicinity of Manassas Junction said property &
> so forth being in charge of the Regimental quartermaster.[138]

Robert Edwards was promoted to Corporal sometime between June 30, 1862, and October 31, 1862. In late September or early October, the 109th Regiment went into camp at Bolivar Heights, Virginia (today West Virginia) on the cliffs directly above Harper's Ferry where it stayed until December 2, 1862. It was there that Robert Edwards deserted from his Regiment on November 16, 1862. He only served 8-1/2 months of his three year term.

Exactly why Robert Edwards deserted is not stated in his military record. Harper's Ferry was a sensitive area located at the confluence of the Shenandoah and the Potomac Rivers, where the B&O Railroad, so vital to the Union army defenses, crossed the Potomac.[139] That there were numerous problems concerning the Union troops stationed in and around Harper's Ferry during this period is indisputable as evidenced by the following excerpt from a letter written to Secretary of War Stanton two days before Robert Edwards deserted:

> I find the statements from the Valley of Virginia are hourly becoming more
> definite and serious. ... I feel it a duty to advise that the forces at Harper's Ferry
> are reported to be generally not well disciplined and effective; and that the
> enemy are believed to be moving in that vicinity also for another attack on that
> point. I beg to suggest that you have the fortifications and forces at Harper's
> Ferry promptly examined. The best troops and increased numbers may soon be

necessary there to maintain a successful defense. I trust your superior facilities may enable you to obtain full and reliable information regarding these important subjects, and that you may be able, if necessary, to take such prompt and vigorous action from the west and east as will prevent renewed and most grave disasters.[140]

After deserting his Regiment, Robert Edwards probably returned directly to Philadelphia. He may, in fact, have hidden aboard one of the trains operated by the B&O Railroad that ran over the tracks from Harper's Ferry, via Baltimore, to Philadelphia. In any event, on January 13, 1863, the record indicates that even though he was known to be a deserter from the 109th Regiment, he enrolled as a Private in Company F of the 156th Regiment of the Pennsylvania Volunteer Infantry for a three year term.[141]

Confirmation of Robert Edwards' enrollment in the 156th Regiment is contained in a cryptic notation in his compiled military service record for the 109th Regiment that says:

> [Robert Edwards was] known to be in Co. I (sic) 156 Regt P.V. Colonel Ernwein (sic).[142] Capt. Farran knew him [i.e., Robert Edwards] to be a deserter when he enlisted him for Co. I (sic) 156th P.V.[143]

Why Robert Edwards was not arrested forthwith for desertion upon his return to Philadelphia is unclear since it is obvious that his whereabouts were known. The only explanation may be contained in an article that appeared in the *Philadelphia Public Ledger* on November 4, 1862, to the effect that:

> The attention of the proper military authorities should be directed to the number of deserters who dressed in citizens' clothing, are daily seen walking the streets of the city. The number of deserters from Burns' brigade, published in the Ledger last week, is large, but it does not include all who have deserted from that brigade. A number of soldiers have left since that list was made up. Two weeks ago, a lieutenant and a number of men deserted from one of the regiments and have not since been arrested although the officers must be aware of their residence and absence from duty. One reason assigned for these desertions is that so many of the officers are absent from their companies that the men have become careless and lax in their discipline. While the officers thus show such utter dereliction of duty, the men cannot be expected to be much better.[144]

Recruitment for the 156th Regiment was poor so the recruits, amounting to about a company, were consolidated with the 157th Regiment on February 27, 1863.[145] However, there is no evidence that Robert Edwards ever made the move to the 157th Regiment.

So, at the end of the war, Robert Edwards was not accounted for in the official records of the Union army.

THE NATURALIZATION OF ROBERT EDWARDS. Although the first enumeration of the 1870 census states that Robert Edwards was a male citizen of the United States eligible to vote, no trace of his naturalization has ever been found in the city or county courts of Philadelphia, the

Supreme Court of Pennsylvania, or in the United States District Court for the Eastern District of Pennsylvania.[146]

MARRIAGE TO ELIZABETH CUSACK. Robert Edwards married his first wife, Elizabeth Cusack, on February 5, 1863, at the Church of the Redemption, a Protestant Episcopal church located at 400 N. 22nd Street.[147,148] The Reverend George A. Durborrow officiated at the ceremony. At the time of their marriage, Robert was 21 and Elizabeth Cusack (who was born in Kentucky) was said to be 16 (sic).

Unfortunately, Elizabeth "Lizzie" (Cusack) Edwards did not live very long after she and Robert Edwards were married. According to the 1865 Death Register for the City of Philadelphia, she died on August 9, 1865 during a smallpox epidemic that swept the city.[149,150] Her age was recorded in the death register as 20 (sic) and her place of birth as Philadelphia (sic). She was reported to have been living at Williams Street (now 24th Street) above Brown (in the 15th Ward of the city) at the time she died. She was buried in the same plot as her brother-in-law, George Edwards, and her mother-in-law, Isabella (Scott) Edwards Flanagan.[151] No obituary appeared in the *Philadelphia Public Ledger* to commemorate her passing.

MARRIAGE TO ROSE ANN MCFEELY. Robert Edwards appears to have married for a second time on February 2, 1868. Very little is known about his second marriage except that the Marriage Return for the City of Philadelphia says the Reverend George A. Durborrow officiated at the ceremony in which he united in marriage Robert Hunter Edwards, 23, born in Scotland to Rose Ann McFeely (sic), 21, born in Ireland.[152] The corresponding Marriage Register for the Church of the Redemption lists the groom's name as Robert H. Edwards and the bride's name as Rose Ann Feely (sic).[153] No information is included in the Church Marriage Register concerning the names of the parents or the witnesses.

What happened after Robert Edwards and Rose Ann McFeely were married is unclear. In the first enumeration of the 1870 census taken on July 1, 1870, Robert Edwards does not appear to be living with his wife, Rose Ann.[154] Instead, Robert Edwards was enumerated at 1907 Jones Street in the 9th Ward of the city where he was boarding with Henry and Caroline Young, their daughter, Mary, and several other people. In the second enumeration of the 1870 census taken on November 23, 1870, Robert and Rose Ann (McFeely) Edwards were enumerated together at 1505 Pearl Street in a multi-family household that included themselves, the Doherty family and the McCauley family.[155]

No record of Rose Ann (McFeely) Edwards' death has been found in Philadelphia nor did a death notices appear for her in the *Philadelphia Public Ledger* between the time of her marriage in 1868 and 1874. There is, however, a sadly compelling death record for a 21-year-old woman named Rose McFeely who died on June 24, 1870, at Saint Joseph's Hospital.[156] Her obituary appeared in the *Philadelphia Public Ledger* on June 25, 1870 and she was buried in Old Cathedral Cemetery on that same afternoon.[157,158] Rose McFeely's death was preceded by the death of her day-old infant daughter also named Rose McFeely on June 19, 1870.[159] The infant was buried in free ground at Old Cathedral Cemetery on June 20, 1870.[160]

If Rose Ann (McFeeley) Edwards died on June 25, 1870, Robert Edwards was technically required to report her as *living* in the 1870 census because she was alive on June 1, 1870, the official date of the census. Understandably, he was too grief stricken over the loss of his wife to report her living 6 days after her death when the census enumerator arrived at his door.

Nothing more is known about the daily life and domestic activities of Robert and Rose Ann (McFeely) Edwards. A few year later, on July 17, 1874, Robert signed his brother, William Scott Edwards' declaration for an increase in his Civil War pension.[161]

MARRIAGE TO MARY DOUGHERTY. In the 1880 census, Robert Edwards was enumerated at 1614 Lombard Street with a wife named Mary.[162] Apparently, Robert had remarried for a third time about four years earlier as he and his wife, Mary, had a three-year-old daughter named Bella.[163] Undoubtedly, Bella was named after Robert's mother, Isabella (Scott) Edwards Flanagan. Unfortunately, nothing is known about her life. Robert's third wife, Mary, seems to have been a widow because the 1880 census schedule also lists the names of Robert Edwards' five step-children, Edward Dougherty, James Dougherty, John Dougherty, Mary Dougherty, and Thomas Dougherty ranging in age from 17 to 8.

WORK HISTORY. Throughout his adult life, Robert Edwards appears to have worked at a variety of jobs. A compilation of his occupations as contained in city directories and other sources is as follows:

1862	laborer, 1820 Jones Street	1862 City Directory
1862	cooper (i.e., a barrel maker)	Compiled Military Service Record[164]
1867	drayman, r 1725 Moravian Street	1867 City Directory
1867/8	carman, h 1725 Moravian Street	1867/8 City Directory
1868	carter	Marriage to Rose Ann McFeely[165]
1868/9	carman, h 1725 Moravian Street	1868/9 City Directory
1869	boatman, h r 1725 Moravian Street	1869 City Directory
1870	laborer, r 1907 Jones Street	1870 Census - 1st Enumeration[166]
1880	wagon driver, 1614 Lombard Street	1880 Census[167]

THE DEATH OF ROBERT EDWARDS. On May 21, 1881, Robert Edwards' obituary appeared in the *Philadelphia Public Ledger*.[168] It read simply:

EDWARDS, On the 19th inst., Robert H. Edwards, aged 37 years.

The relatives and friends of the family are respectfully invited to attend the funeral on Saturday afternoon at 4 o'clock from the residence of his brother-in-law, George Chambers, No. 2305 Simes Street. To proceed to Mount Moriah Cemetery.

According to the report of his death, he died of delirium tremens.[169] His name appears in the burial register of Trinity Memorial Chapel located at 22nd and Spruce Streets.[170] He was buried in a plot at Mount Moriah Cemetery belonging to George Chambers, his sister's husband.[171] There was no mention in Robert Edwards' obituary of his wife, Mary, or their young daughter, Bella, thus their fate is unknown.

William Scott Edwards - The Civil War Veteran

On August 31, 1861, William Scott Edwards enlisted in Company D of the 23rd Regiment of the Pennsylvania Volunteer Infantry for a three year term.[172] The regiment, known as Birney's Zouaves, was a very strong and popular regiment.[173]

Prior to his enlistment, William Scott Edwards lived at home with his mother, Isabella, her second husband, Andrew Flanagan, and the rest of the family (except his brother George) at 1820 Jones Street.[174] Part of his motivation in enlisting was undoubtedly financial in that the family badly needed the money.

THE TWENTY-THIRD REGIMENT. William Scott Edwards' military service record says he was 5 feet, 10-1/4 inches tall, of light complexion, grey eyes, and dark hair. He enlisted as a Private. Given the information in his military service record, William Scott Edwards was present and participated in most of the activities, marches, campaigns, battles, and skirmishes of the 23rd Regiment of the Pennsylvania Volunteer Infantry over the next three years except for the time he was hospitalized recovering from wounds he received at the Battle of Fair Oaks on May 31, 1862.

The following are highlights of the history of the 23rd Regiment.[175,176] These items document the probable whereabouts and experiences of William Scott Edwards during the course of the Civil War:

August 31, 1861
> The Regiment was organized in Philadelphia, Pennsylvania.

With the Army of the Potomac

September 1861 - March 1862
> The Regiment was transferred to Washington, D.C., attached to the Army of the Potomac, and quartered at Camp Graham four miles north of Washington where they were on duty in defense of Washington building Forts Lincoln, Totten, Stevens, and Cedar Hill.

March 1-15, 1862
> The Regiment advanced on Manassas, Virginia, but turned back when the enemy retreated.

March 26 - May 23, 1862
> The Regiment moved to Alexandria, Virginia, and boarded the steamer Vanderbilt for a voyage to Fort Monroe in defense of the Virginia Peninsula. They first encountered the enemy at Warwick River on April 4 where one man was shot - its first loss. This was followed by the Siege of Yorktown (April 5 - May 4); a forced march to Williamsburg where the regiment encountered heavy artillery fire on

May 5; and operations about Bottom's Bridge (May 20 - 23)

May 23/24, 1862

The Regiment was on reconnaissance toward Richmond, Virginia, where the enemy was met and driven out. The next day, they were engaged in a heavy skirmish to the left of the Richmond Road.

May 31 - June 1, 1862

The Regiment participated in the Battle of Fair Oaks (Seven Pines), Virginia. The Battle of Fair Oaks (Seven Pines) is described as follows with respect to the activities of the Regiment:

The Twenty-third was separated from the rest of the brigade and directed to take position on the Nine Mile Road, west of the railroad. At two o'clock in the afternoon it met the enemy, and drove him back to, and quite through a piece of wood in front. The ground was difficult, the woods swarmed with the enemy, and this the first engagement in which it was under heavy infantry fire; but several charges were successfully made, in which three color bearers were shot and many brave men lost. Late in the afternoon it was hotly attacked, in position beyond the road, and barely escaped capture by a column of the enemy which swept down in the rear. Colonel Neill had his horse shot under him, but fortunately succeeded in retiring to the line of the First Long Island, Colonel Adams, and formed on his right. In this engagement, the loss in killed and wounded was seven officers and 136 men.

In his official report of the Battle, General Keyes reported that:

At a little past two o'clock I ordered Neill's Twenty-third and Rippey's Sixty-first Pennsylvania regiments to move to the support of Casey's right. Neill attacked the enemy twice with great gallantry. In the first attack, the enemy was driven back. In the second attack, under the immediate command of General Couch, these two regiments assailed a vastly superior force of the enemy and fought with extraordinary bravery; though compelled at last to retire, they brought in thirty-five prisoners. Both regiments were badly cut up. After this attack, the Twenty-third took part in the hard fighting which closed the day, near Seven Pines.

The company muster roll card for William Scott Edwards shows that he was absent from the company after the Battle of Fair Oaks having been sent to a hospital in Annapolis, Maryland, for treatment of wounds received in the battle. Further, the company muster roll card shows that he was still absent from the company in July and August having been sent to Philadelphia because of the wound to his left hand.[177] It was during this time that William Scott Edwards' left forefinger was amputated.

September 1862

When the Peninsula Campaign ended, the Regiment returned to Alexandria, Virginia. William Scott Edwards probably rejoined the Regiment at this point just in time for the Maryland Campaign.

September - October 1862

The Regiment participated in the Maryland Campaign. They guarded the Potomac from White's Ford to Nolans's Ferry during the battles of South Mountain and Antietam (September 11-24); then they moved to Downsville on September 24 where they stood picket duty on the Potomac until November 1.

November 1-19, 1862

The Regiment moved to Falmouth, Virginia, where it skirmished daily with the enemy.

December 12-15, 1862

The Regiment was heavily engaged in the Battle of Fredericksburg where it was placed in the advance and ordered to seize the Stone House. The enemy fell back, the line moved forward, and the pickets were established.

January 20-24, 1863

The Regiment participated in a useless "mud march" to United States Ford where it expected to be engaged in a bloody campaign on the right bank of the Rappahannock River. After turning back, it made winter quarters in Falmouth until April.

It was at Falmouth, according to a statement made by Lieutenant William Vogdes, Jr., on September 10, 1864, that William Scott Edwards first contracted a cold during the month of January that settled in his lungs and plagued him continually thereafter.[178]

April 27-May 6, 1863

The Regiment participated in the Chancellorsville Campaign where they successfully carried pontoon boats on their backs for two miles in order to quietly make a landing and surprise the enemy. The Regiment also participated in operations at Franklin's Crossing from April 29 to May 2; Fredericksburg and Marye's Heights on May 3 which is described as follows:

The Twenty-third Regiment was not in the storming party, having already done its work; but seeing a regiment whose term of service had expired break at the moment of extreme peril, the men of the Twenty-third, without orders, giving one grand huzzah, started upon the run for the opening in the broken line and entered the works with the triumphant column.

One hundred silver medals were awarded in September to the heroic enlisted men of the Regiment who participated in the bayonet charge at Marye's Heights.

A severe engagement at Salem Heights followed. The enemy attack was so strong, the Regiment was forced to retreat to Bank's Ford on May 4. Another line of battle was reformed, but the Regiment was finally forced to recross the river and return to Falmouth.

June 6-13, 1863

The Regiment crossed to the south side of the river at Deep Run Ravine. It was placed on the skirmish line close up to the enemy's front where it encountered heavy skirmishing with considerable loss. Recrossing the river after June 13, the Regiment started its long march toward Gettysburg. The weather was extremely hot and the march was at times forced.

July 2-4, 1863

The Regiment arrived on the battlefield at Gettysburg at four o'clock on the afternoon of July 2. Its activities at Gettysburg are described as follows:

Forming in a mass, it started at a double quick, every man cheering to the full capacity of his lungs. The enemy, dispirited by the appearance of fresh troops, soon fell back. On the morning of the 3rd, the Twenty-third was ordered to reinforce General Geary. At ten o'clock, the Twenty-third was ordered forward as skirmishers to test the lull in the enemy's fire. The right wing advanced about fifteen paces when they were met with so terrific a fire that they were compelled to lie down under protection of the line occupying the Union breastworks. Soon thereafter, they fell back to the line where they remained until relieved by troops from Ohio. Soon after, the Twenty-third was again ordered forward to reinforce the left center upon which the whole rebel fire was concentrated. In executing this order, the Twenty-third was compelled to cross an open plain under as heavy a fire of artillery as ever rocked a battlefield. After marching from point to point during the [remainder of the] day, the Regiment finally rested for the night. On July 4, the Regiment spent the day skirmishing with the enemy, bringing in the wounded, and burying the dead.

William Scott Edwards' mother, Isabella (Scott) Edwards Flanagan, died on July 25, 1863, probably without ever knowing whether her son was one of the 23,000 Union casualties (killed, wounded, captured, or missing) of the Battle of Gettysburg. Undoubtedly, it was also quite some time before he learned of her untimely death.

August - September, 1863

The Regiment moved to Warrenton and Culpepper, Virginia, where it was reinforced and posted as guard to the Alexandria and Orange Railroad.

October 9-22, 1863

The Regiment marched to Centreville and formed in line of battle at Bristoe Station, Virginia. From there it moved to Chantilly and reformed in line. The rebel army withdrew.

November 7-8, 1863

The Regiment advanced to the Rappahannock River where it was in line during the brilliant battle at that place resulting in the capture of two thousand prisoners with their small arms, several colors, and four pieces of artillery.

November 16 - December 2, 1863

The Regiment crossed the Rapidan River on November 13 and was assigned to support Gregg's Cavalry during the Mine Run Campaign. The Regiment was told to prepare for a charge at eight o'clock on November 30, but the charge was never made and the Regiment lay exposed to intense cold without heat from any fire until the night of December 1 when it fell back, recrossed the river, and returned to its old camp.

December 30, 1963

The veteran volunteers reenlisted on December 30, 1863, and went on furlough to Philadelphia until February 11, 1864. William Scott Edwards was not among the veteran volunteers. He remained in camp. The company muster roll card shows that in February 1864 William Scott Edwards was promoted to Corporal vice Washington O. Moore who was reduced in rank.[179]

During this time, the friends of the Regiment in Philadelphia gave a ball for its benefit. With the proceeds, they bought 600 pairs of woolen gloves and a beautiful stand of colors bearing the names of all the battles in which the Regiment had participated. Earlier, the patriotic ladies of Bucks County had bought ear-comforters for the men.

Johnson's Island, Sandusky, Ohio

January 6 - May 6, 1864

The Regiment moved to Johnson's Island on Lake Erie in Ohio where the men guarded rebel prisoners at that place until May 6.

With the Army of the Potomac

May 9-23, 1964

The Regiment moved to Washington, D.C., then to Belle Plains during the Wilderness Campaign where it guarded rebel prisoners and escorted supply trains containing 500 wagons to the front lines. After delivering the supply trains, the Regiment crossed the North Anna River and, after a hard march, reached its destination where it commenced to destroy the Virginia Central Railroad by burning ties, heating and twisting rails, and demolishing bridges.

May 23 - June 12, 1864

The Regiment recrossed the North Anna River for the Rapidan Campaign. It arrived on June 1 at Cold Harbor, a place that is associated with bitter memories for the Regiment. The 23rd Regiment was selected to storm the enemy's lines which were located on a hill 500 yards away beyond an open field. The open field had to be crossed without shelter. The charge across the open field and the twenty-five minutes of hand-to-hand fighting on the enemy side left few men in the Regiment able to return to their place on the line. On the night of June 2, a torrential rain began to fall. Heavy fire from the enemy continued from then until the night of June 12 when the attempt to break through to the enemy's lines was abandoned.

It is here that William Scott Edwards claimed to have been shot in the left leg and/or contracted pleurisy.[180]

June 17 - July 9, 1864

Marching and countermarching, the Regiment finally arrived at the James River on June 16 and boarded the steamer Cauliflower where it sailed for Bermuda Hundred. After landing, it was ordered into line of battle across the Appomattox River in front of Petersburg (June 17/19). An attempt was made to move forward in the face of murderous infantry fire. Later, the Regiment was ordered to march to Ream's Station on the Weldon Railroad where it was immediately placed on the picket line (June 22/23). On July 2, the Regiment returned to its former position just in time to participate in the Siege of Petersburg (July 9)

July 9-12, 1864

> On July 9, the Regiment was reassigned to the Army of the Shenandoah and moved to Washington to repulse Early's attack on Washington

July 14-18, 1864

> The Regiment participated in the Snicker's Gap Expedition. It crossed the Potomac at White's Ford, marched to Leesburg, and then passed through Snicker's Gap where it went into line of battle on the mountain near the Shenandoah River. Being in an exposed position, however, the Regiment moved to the right, forded the Shenandoah River, and marched out on the Winchester Pike.

August 1864

> Operations continued in the Shenandoah Valley. By now, the men of the Regiment were worn out with marching and countermarching. The heat was intense and large numbers suffered from sun stroke. On August 21, the Regiment was surprised at Charlestown, West Virginia, and only after much fighting and considerable loss did they regain the ground. Thankfully, the term of the Regiment was now expired and William Scott Edwards was ordered home to Philadelphia to be mustered out. He arrived in Philadelphia on August 25 with the Regiment.

September 8, 1864

> The company muster-out roll card shows that Corporal William Scott Edwards was released from the Regiment in Philadelphia on September 8, 1864. At that time, he was due $5.32 for clothing and $100.00, possibly a bounty payment.[181]

BECOMING A CITIZEN. William Scott Edward was a very busy man after his release from the 23rd Regiment. He immediately submitted a petition for naturalization which took place in the District Court for the City and County of Philadelphia on September 30, 1864.[182] His witness was Alexander Kelly with whose family the Edwards shared a house in 1860.

APPLYING FOR A CIVIL WAR PENSION. Within two days of his release from the 23rd Regiment, William Scott Edwards filed for a Civil War invalid pension. He was examined by Surgeon H. Lewis Hodge who found him to be one-quarter disabled due to the amputation of his left forefinger. He was also found to be suffering from chronic pleurisy. As a result, on December 1, 1864, he was awarded a pension by the Adjutant General's Office of $2.00 per month payable quarterly retroactive to September 8, 1864.[183,184]

MARRIAGE TO JANE MARTIN. William Scott Edwards may have married for the first time in 1864. The evidence of this marriage is the following intriguing answer he provided, in writing, to a question posed by the Bureau of Pensions in January 1898 concerning any prior marriages:

> I was married to Miss Jany Mardin (sic) who died July 4 1864 (sic) no children.[185]

This information is difficult to interpret. As best can be determined by an examination of William Scott Edwards' military and pension files, he was not in Philadelphia in July 1864.

WORK HISTORY. According to William Scott Edwards' Civil War pension file, he was working as a porter bottler at the time of his enlistment in the 23rd Regiment and he resumed that work in 1864 after he was discharged from the military.[186,187]

In his original Application for an Invalid Army Pension dated September 10, 1864, William Scott Edwards indicates that he was living at 1920 Jones Street. Assuming he was, in fact, married on July 4, 1864, his household likely would have consisted of his wife, Jane (Martin) Edwards, his step-father, Andrew Flanagan, and possibly his brother, Robert Edwards and his wife, Elizabeth (Cusack) Edwards, but not his sister, Annie Adam Edwards who was residing with the family of John Freed, Cork Merchant, at 2326 or 2328 Market Street or his brother, George Edwards who was living nearby at the rear of 1907 Jones Street.[188]

About 1866, William Scott Edwards, his wife, Jane, and possibly Andrew Flanagan, moved from 1920 Jones Street to the rear of 1725 Moravian Street where William continued to support the family working as a porter bottler. William Scott Edwards and his wife, Jane, were listed together at that location in the first enumeration of the 1870 census.[189] In the second enumeration, Andrew Flanagan was listed with them.[190] After Jane (Martin) Edwards died in 1873, William Scott Edwards moved to 2516 Pine Street where he continued working as a bottler until sometime later in his life when he claimed in a deposition contained in his pension file to have worked as a switch cleaner for the Philadelphia Rapid Transit Company. By 1890, he was listed in the Philadelphia city directory as a watchman, work which he continued performing until at least 1900.[191] By the time of the 1910 census, he was finally retired.[192]

Thus, William Scott Edwards worked hard all his adult life to support his family, both immediate and extended.

THE DEATH OF JANE (MARTIN) EDWARDS. Jane (Martin) Edwards died on October 10, 1873 of meningitis.[193] Her obituary, which appeared in the *Philadelphia Public Ledger*, read as follows:

> EDWARDS, On the 10th inst., JANE, wife of William Edwards, aged 32 years.
>
> The relatives and friends of the family are respectfully invited to attend the funeral this (Monday) afternoon at 1 o'clock from the residence of her mother, Mrs. Ann Lamb, No. 3133 Ludlow st., below Market, West Philadelphia. To proceed to Cathedral Cemetery.[194]

She was buried in Old Cathedral Cemetery in a family plot that belonged to William J. Martin.[195] According to William Scott Edwards' pension file, they had no children.

MARRIAGE TO ROSE CLARK. William Scott Edwards married Rose Clark at Saint Charles Borromeo Roman Catholic Church on August 19, 1875. The marriage was solemnized by Rev. J. O'Reilly.[196,197,198] Rose Clark was the daughter of Thomas and Ann Clark.

MARRIED LIFE AT 2502 PINE STREET. Together, William Scott and Rose (Clark) Edwards had nine children over a period of 13 years. All of their children were baptized at Saint Patrick's Roman Catholic Church.[199] By all indications, they lived together happily at 2502 Pine Street surrounded by their children and members of the Clark family who either lived with them or elsewhere in the 2500 block of Pine Street.[200,201,202,203] William Scott Edwards also remained in frequent contact with his sister, Annie Adam Edwards, who was married to George Washington Chambers.

Sadly, only five of their nine children appear to have reached their majority.[204]

CONVERSION TO ROMAN CATHOLICISM. William Scott Edwards converted to Roman Catholicism on June 18, 1893, at Saint Patrick's Roman Catholic Church.[205] After his conversion, he may have changed his name to William Joseph Edwards.

JOINING THE GRAND ARMY OF THE REPUBLIC. William Scott Edwards joined the Grand Army of the Republic (GAR) on June 8, 1887.[206] He was a member of General D.B. Birney Post, No. 63, which met at Germantown Avenue and Diamond Street on Wednesday. There is reported to be a small triangular park at the site of the Post named for General Birney.

The GAR was a secret semi-military order.[207] The requirements for membership were that the candidate hold an honorable discharge from the army or navy of the United States. It was organized soon after the close of the Civil War for the purpose of continuing the associations formed among the soldiers and sailors, to care for comrades in distress or their widows and orphans, and to serve the government in any emergency where it might be called upon. Its aims were expressed in its motto of Fraternity, Charity and Loyalty. Apparently, many of the men who took a prominent part in the political movements of soldiers and sailors in 1865 and 1866 were also prominent in the formation of the GAR. As this partisanship caused significant internal problems, the GAR was reorganized in 1869 and 1870 and all political and partisan action in any form was prohibited.

Since membership was restricted to those who served the Union in the Civil War, this organization no longer exists today.

THE DEATH OF ROSE (CLARK) EDWARDS. Rose (Clark) Edwards died of pulmonary congestion on February 15, 1907, at the age of 60.[208] Her obituary read as follows:

> EDWARDS - On February 15, 1907, ROSE, wife of William Edwards, Sr.
> Relatives and friends are invited to attend the funeral on Tuesday at 8:30 a.m.
> from her late residence, 2502 Pine Street. High Mass of Requiem at St. Patrick's
> Church. Interment at Cathedral Cemetery.[209]

She was laid to rest in the plot belonging to her brother, John Clark, at Old Cathedral

Cemetery alongside her four children who died in infancy or early childhood and her son, Thomas, who died on September 25, 1905, at the age of 26.[210]

THE DEATH OF WILLIAM SCOTT EDWARDS. William Scott Edwards followed his wife in death four years later after a long life that was punctuated by **frequent** requests for increases in his Civil War pension. He was 71 years old at the time of his death from myocarditis.[211] His obituary read as follows:

> EDWARDS, On January 7, 1911, William S. Edwards, husband of the late Rose Edwards (nee Clark). Relatives and friends also Post 63 of the GAR are invited to attend the funeral on Wednesday at 8:30 A.M. from his late residence at 2502 Pine Street. High Mass of Requiem at St. Patrick's Church at 10 A.M. Interment at Cathedral Cemetery.[212]

True to his Scottish heritage, William Scott Edwards' ingenuity and persistence resulted in an average annual increase in his Civil War pension of 3.89 percent. In fact, when he died in 1911, he was being paid a disability benefit of $12.00 per month payable quarterly.[213] The payment would have been higher had he not experienced some difficulty in 1910 trying to convince a Special Government Investigator that he was born in Philadelphia in 1837 which would have entitled him to a pension increase due to his age. The irony of his final rejected request for an increase in his Civil War pension is that it resulted in a rich collection of family history information being compiled by the government investigator in pursuit of the correct birth date and place of William Scott Edwards.[214]

William Scott Edwards is buried in Old Cathedral Cemetery alongside his wife, Rose (Clark) Edwards, and five of their children.[215]

THE PENNSYLVANIA MEMORIAL AT GETTYSBURG. To commemorate the sacrifice of those men from Pennsylvania who fought in one of the bloodiest battles of the Civil War, the State of Pennsylvania built a large memorial in Gettysburg on Cemetery Ridge. The monument itself is 70 feet tall and made of Pennsylvania Mount Airy granite and bronze from battlefield cannons.

The memorial was dedicated on September 27, 1910, just three months before William Scott Edwards died. His name is proudly inscribed on the wall of the memorial along with the names of all the other Pennsylvania volunteers who took part in the battle including that of his step-father, Andrew Flanagan.

Annie Adam (Edwards) Chambers - The Only Daughter

Annie Adam Edwards was remembered by her great-granddaughter, the late Josephine (Thompson) Marshall, as a tall slender woman with a thick accent.[216] She had a take-charge personality and she prided herself in her good memory even though her recollection of dates was somewhat inexact.

MARRIAGE TO GEORGE WASHINGTON CHAMBERS. Annie Adam Edwards married George Washington Chambers on July 4, 1866, at the Church of the Redemption.[217,218,219] The ceremony was performed by the Reverend George A. Durborrow of the Protestant Episcopal Church located at 22nd and Callowhill. Annie was 19 years old when they married and George was 25.

The day Annie Adam Edwards and George Washington Chambers were married was a very important day in Philadelphia as it was the day that Pennsylvania officially closed its records on the Civil War. To quote the *Philadelphia Public Ledger*:

> Her [Pennsylvania's] flags, carried thousands of miles by her sons, and always borne side by side with the foremost in the strife, were on that day returned to the State, to remain as glorious memorials of Pennsylvania's devotion to the Union.
>
> Every train reaching Philadelphia, commencing as early as Sunday evening and continuing as late as Wednesday morning, was filled to its utmost capacity.
>
> At daybreak the national salutes announced the advent of the Fourth of July, and the citizens prepared to give the finishing touches to decorations commenced previously. Everywhere the display of bunting was profuse. The national colors were thrown to the breeze from flagstaffs and windows, or were used to decorate the fronts of houses. and the result was that on all the main thoroughfares and especially on the streets on the route of the parade, the "red, white and blue" were the predominating colors, and gave to the city a gala appearance such as has rarely heretofore been witnessed. It was truly a flag-jubilee, and every individual seemed to consider it his individual duty to assist to the full extent of his power in making the day one long to be remembered. The number of magnificent displays at private dwellings exceeded any previous attempt in this city, while the larger stores on Chestnut and Arch Streets made displays of corresponding magnificence.
>
> At ten o'clock, a detachment of mounted police moved forward leading a procession of seven military divisions comprised of Regiments that represented Pennsylvania during the War of the Rebellion. The reception for the flags took place at Independence Square and was very impressive. After this ceremony, General Henry White, chairman of the committee of arrangements, made a brief address. After a prayer by Reverend Doctor Brainerd, General Meade advanced with the colors of the Eighty-second Regiment in his hand, and in a formal address delivered them to Governor Curtin. Governor Curtin then made a brief reply and received the flags on behalf of the State. The meeting was adjourned with a benediction by Bishop Simpson.[220]

It was undoubtedly a glorious and memorable day to be married.

THE EARLY YEARS. Little is known of Annie Adam Edwards life before her marriage. In a sworn statement she gave before a notary public on February 15, 1917, in connection with a request for an increase in her Civil War widow's pension she claimed to have been born on February 26, 1847, in Scotland.[221] To substantiate her claim, she presented the Edwards Family

Bible which contained a corresponding entry concerning her date of birth.

At the time of the 1850 census, Annie Adam Edwards can be found living in the Spring Garden Ward 4 with her widowed mother, Isabella, and her four brothers - George, William, Robert and Joseph.[222] A month later, Annie Adam Edwards was re-enumerated in North Mulberry Ward with both her parents and her four brothers - George, William, Robert, and Joseph.[223] The precise reason for the re-enumeration is unknown.

Exactly what happened to the family in the years immediately following th death of Annie's father in 1850 is unknown. Later, however, in another sworn statement given on March 19, 1917, she said that:

> ...she resided with her mother and three brothers George, William, and Robert Edwards on Jones Street between 18th and 19th Streets, in the 9th Ward of the City of Philadelphia between the years 1858 and 1862. [She] resided at # 3 Curry's Court which ran off Jones Street between 19th and 20th Streets and Market and Filbert Streets in the said Ward and City between the years 1862 and 1864. From 1864 to 1866 [she] resided with the family of John Freed, Cork Merchant [at] 2326 or 2328 Market Street, Philadelphia.[224]

WIFE AND MOTHER. Annie Adam (Edwards) Chambers further indicated in her sworn statement of March 19, 1917, that after she and George Washington Chambers were married on July 4, 1866, they moved to 2301 Simes Street where they lived with John Clark and his family. What she failed to mention in her statement was that John Clark was her husband's brother-in-law in that he was married to George Washington Chambers' sister, Emma.[225,226]

On June 5, 1867, George and Annie Adam (Edwards) Chambers' first child was born.[227] Annie named her first child William Scott Chambers. Most likely she named her son after her brother, William Scott Edwards, in honor of his determination, tenacity, and continuous hard work, from the time he was very young, throughout some very difficult years, to help support their mother, Isabella (Scott) Edwards Flanagan, his brothers, his sister, and his step-father, Andrew Flanagan.

Their second child, a daughter named Eliza Jane, was born on October 23, 1869.[228] After whom the baby may have been named is unclear. In any case, the two oldest children were baptized at the Church of the Redemption on January 12, 1868, and January 9, 1870, respectively.[229]

Annie claimed in her sworn statement of March 19, 1917, that she "went to housekeeping in the year 1869 on Race Street between 23rd and 24th, and resided there until 1871." This is consistent with the 1870 census which shows that by June 28, 1870, the Chambers family had moved from 2301 Simes Street to 2302 Race Street.[230,231] This move may have been in connection with George Washington Chambers taking a job as a driver.

Sometime in 1871, the family moved again. This was a move away from the wharfs along the Schuylkill River to a neighborhood in North Philadelphia known as Brewerytown. Their house was located in the vicinity of several beer breweries including the Bergdoll and Psotta Brewing Company and the Bergner and Engel Brewing Company. Their new address is included in the obituary of their baby daughter, Eliza Jane, who died unexpectedly on November 18, 1871. Her obituary appeared in the *Philadelphia Public Ledger* as follows:

> CHAMBERS - On the 18th inst., of inflammation of the lungs, Eliza Jane, daughter of George W. and Annie A. Chambers, age 2 years, 25 days. The relatives and friends of the family are respectfully invited to attend the funeral from the residence of her parents 2627 Mt. Pleasant (west of Girard College) on Tuesday afternoon at 1 o'clock. Interment at Mt. Moriah Cemetery.[232]

When their daughter died, George Washington and Annie Adam (Edwards) Chambers bought a plot at Mount Moriah Cemetery where Eliza Jane Chambers was laid to rest.[233]

Life went on. George Washington and Annie Adam (Edwards) Chambers eventually moved back to Simes Street (known as Ludlow Street after 1897) where they rented a house at 2305, two doors away from John and Emma (Chambers) Clark who were still living at 2301 Simes Street.[234,235] George appears to have returned to work as a boatman. The family may even have resumed attending the Church of the Redemption because the late Josephine (Thompson) Marshall recalled that her grandfather, William Scott Chambers, once told her that as a child he was a member of the Episcopal Church choir.[236]

Their daughters, Lydia, Emma, and Annie were born on February 27, 1872, March 23, 1875, and February 12, 1878, respectively.[237] It is unclear why Annie named her second daughter Lydia, but Emma was undoubtedly named after George's sister, Emma (Chambers) Clark and Annie was probably named after her mother.

Their second son, George Edwards Chambers, was born on July 1, 1880.[238] He could have been named after his father, or his paternal grandfather, or maybe even Annie's oldest brother, George Edwards. Lastly, Elizabeth, fondly known as Bessie, was born on September 1, 1883.[239] She was probably named for George Washington Chambers' mother.

Because George Washington Chambers worked as a boatman for most of their married life, the family spent many years living in Center City Philadelphia in the immediate vicinity of 23rd and Market and Chestnut Streets on the east side of the Schuylkill River. This put George Washington Chambers within easy walking distance of the wharfs where he worked.

For reasons unknown, George Washington and Annie Adam (Edwards) Chambers made another big move in about 1889 when they relocated the family across the river to West Philadelphia. At first they resided at 3211 St. James Place.[240] After 1894, they moved a few blocks away to 3223 Lombard Street (also known as Marston Street prior to 1897).[241] Both of these addresses were within easy walking distance of the wharfs on the west side of the Schuylkill River.

THE CHARACTER OF ANNIE ADAM (EDWARDS) CHAMBERS. While George Washington Chambers continued to work tirelessly to support his family by loading and unloading ships and schooners at wharfs along the Schuylkill River, Annie kept busy keeping house and tending to the needs of her entire family - both immediate and extended. For richer or for poorer, in sickness and in health, she was always there to help her family. She even took care of funeral and burial arrangements for her brother, Robert Edwards who died in 1881; her granddaughter, Annie Chambers, (the child of her youngest son, George Edwards Chambers) who was stillborn in 1907, and her married daughter, Elizabeth (Chambers) McManus who died in 1911. All three family members were buried by Annie in the Chambers family plot at Mount Moriah Cemetery alongside Eliza Jane Chambers, her baby daughter who died in infancy may years earlier.[242]

In addition to her many duties and responsibilities as wife and mother, Annie was the single source of information about the family's oral tradition. She knew the details of her family's life in Scotland as told to her by her mother, Isabella, and she had in her possession her parents' original marriage certificate and the Edwards Family Bible.[243,244] She prided herself in her recollection of dates and events. As proof thereof, she gave countless depositions and sworn statements over the years in support of (or, in one case, in apparent contradiction of) her husband's, her brother's, and her own requests for increases in their Civil War pensions.

She was a true and loyal wife to George Washington Chambers for all 40 years of their marriage.

WIDOWHOOD. After the death of George Washington Chambers in 1906, Annie applied for a Civil War widow's pension.[245,246] The pension was granted and, over the years, gradually increased to a grand total of $30.00 per month payable quarterly.[247]

Annie eventually went to live with her married daughter, Emma (Chambers) Spence at 2823 Wharton Street in South Philadelphia. It was from that address that she may have looked up into the night sky on the evening of April 20, 1910, and seen the return of Halley's comet.

Later, Annie moved with the Spence family to 2417 S. 61st Street in West Philadelphia. It was while she was living at that address that her oldest granddaughter, Lucy (Chambers) Thompson, died of tuberculosis on November 22, 1918, just as the city was finally emerging from the grip of the world-wide influenza epidemic. It was also at that address where she anxiously awaited the return of her oldest grandson, Henry Grafe Chambers, from his service in the U.S. Navy during World War I.

Sometime after 1920, as the nation ushered in prohibition and the decade of the Roaring Twenties with its inconceivable changes in women's fashion and hairstyles, Annie quietly moved with the Spence family to 7119 Upland Street in West Philadelphia. Although she lived with the Spence family for the rest of her life, she continued to visit frequently with her other children, her grandchildren, and her great-grandchildren as well as with the children of her brother, William Scott Edwards, who died in 1911.

In fact, Annie's great-granddaughter, the late Josephine (Thompson) Marshall, recalled that her great-grandmother often visited William Scott Chambers (her oldest son) and his wife, Josephine (Reitze) Chambers, when they lived at 5313 Yocum Street. At the conclusion of each visit, William Scott Chambers would invariably escort his mother to the trolley car stop, help her get aboard, and then, despite her protestations, jump onto the trolley car at the very last minute and ride with her all the way home.[248]

THE DEATH OF ANNIE ADAM (EDWARDS) CHAMBERS. Annie Adam (Edwards) Chambers, the force that bound her family together, died of arteriosclerosis on December 27, 1927, at the age of 80.[249] Her great-grandson, the late William Scott Chambers, remembered attending her funeral when he was only six-and-a-half years old.[250]

She was buried alongside her husband, George Washington Chambers, and other members of the family in the Chambers family plot at Mount Moriah Cemetery.[251] Sadly, no obituary appeared in the Philadelphia newspapers to commemorate her passing.

ENDNOTES

1.The family surname appears as both Edward or Edwards in original records created as early as 1806. For simplicity, the surname is written as Edwards in almost all instances in this family history.

2.Old Parochial Registers of Scotland, Edinburgh, Midlothian, Scotland, St. Cuthbert's Church, Marriages (includes index), 1833-1841, FHL Microfilm Roll 1066765, Item2, contains the marriage record of Adam Edwards and Isabella Scott dated December 28, 1838, stating he lived at No. 3 Warriston Street (sic) and she lived on Canon Street in Canonmills. Also, 1841 Scotland Census, Midlothian, Edinburgh St Cuthbert's Parish; ED 20A; page 7; line 1250, <<www.ancestry.com>>, downloaded January 29, 2016, states their address was No. 3 Canon Street. Canonmills was in the Second New Town of Edinburgh.

3.John Keay and Julia Keay, *Collins Encyclopedia of Scotland*, (London: Harper Collins Publishers, 1994), 286.

4.Old Parochial Registers of Scotland, Galashiels, Selkirk, Parish Church of Galashiels, Baptisms, 1714-1854, FHL Microfilm Roll 1067925, Items 2-4, contains the baptismal record of Isabella Scott dated June 17, 1818.

5.Old Parochial Registers of Scotland, Edinburgh, Midlothian, Scotland, St. Cuthbert's Church, Marriages (includes index), 1833-1841, FHL Microfilm Roll 1066765, Item 2, contains the marriage record of Adam Edwards and Isabella Scott dated December 28, 1838, stating her father, William Scott, was a farm servant in Pebbles.

6.James G. Leyburn, *The Scotch-Irish- A Social History*, (Chapel Hill, North Carolina: The University of North Carolina Press, 1962), 8.

7.Leyburn, 65.

8.Leyburn, 68.

9.Leyburn, 71.

10.Samuel Lewis, *Topographical Dictionary of Scotland, Comprising the Several Counties, Islands, Cities, Burgh and Market Towns, Parishes, and Principal Villages, with Historical and Statistical Descriptions - Second Edition*, (London, 1851, reprint: Baltimore, Maryland: Genealogical Publishing Company, 1989), Volume II:459.

11.The Duke of Buccleuch is the Chief of Clan Scott. The Dukes of Buccleuch descend from Sir Richard the Scott (1249-1285) and from Sir Walter Scott to whom James II granted lands in Selkirkshire in 1452. The Dukedom dates from 1663. The family seat of Bowhill remains in Selkirk to this day

12.Lewis, Volume II:459.

13.Lewis, Volume II:460.

14.Lewis, Volume II:457.

15. Old Parochial Registers of Scotland, Selkirk, Selkirk, Parish Church of Selkirk, Marriages, 1719-1854, FHL Microfilm Roll 1067928, contains the marriage record of William Scott and Anne Brown dated June 15, 1810.

16.Old Parochial Registers of Scotland, Selkirk, Selkirk, Parish Church of Selkirk, Baptisms, 1766-1854, FHL Microfilm Roll 1067928, contains the baptismal record of William Scott dated May 17, 1786.

17.Old Parochial Registers of Scotland, Selkirk, Selkirk, Parish Church of Selkirk, Baptisms, 1766-1854, FHL Microfilm Roll 1067928, contains the baptismal record of Anne Brown dated October 2, 1791.

18.Old Parochial Registers of Scotland, Galashiels, Selkirk, Parish Church of Galashiels, Baptisms, 1714-1854, FHL Microfilm Roll 1067925, Items 2-4, contains the baptismal record of Isabella Scott dated June 17, 1818.

19.Old Parochial Registers of Scotland, Galashiels, Selkirk, Parish Church of Galashiels, Baptisms, 1714-1854, FHL Microfilm Roll 1067925, Items 2-4, contains the baptismal record of Andrew Scott dated January 15, 1821 and William Scott dated February 6, 1825.

20.Lewis, Volume I:475.

21.Keay and Keay, 410.

22.Lewis, Volume I:476.

23.Lewis, Volume I:476.

24.Keay and Keay, 410.

25.Keay and Keay, 410.

26.Keay and Keay, 505.

27.The Duke of Buccleuch is the Chief of Clan Scott.

28.Old Parochial Registers of Scotland, Edinburgh, Midlothian, Scotland, St. Cuthbert's Church, Baptisms (includes index), 1820-1826, FHL Microfilm Roll 0993529 contains the birth record of Adam Edwards dated October 22, 1820.

29.Keay and Keay, 157.

30.Keay and Keay, 203. Culdees were monastic groups that existed in the Celtic era Churches of Scotland and Ireland in isolated pockets as late as the 14th Century. They were organized around secular hereditary priests. They eventually died out or were absorbed by subsequent parishes.

31.Keay and Keay, 331.

32.Old Parochial Registers of Scotland, Edinburgh, Midlothian, Scotland, St. Cuthbert's Church, Marriages, 1788-1818, Microfilm Roll 1066757, contains the Banns Matrimonial of George Edwards and Agnes Adam, daughter of John Adam of Dundee, dated May 17, 1806.

33.Old Parochial Registers of Scotland, Edinburgh, Midlothian, Scotland, St. Cuthbert's Church, Marriages (includes index), 1833-1841, FHL Microfilm Roll 1066765, Item 1, contains the marriage record of Alexander Edwards and Margaret McIntosh, daughter of the late Peter McIntosh, smith at Kinloch in the Parish of Rannoch, Perthshire, dated April 6, 1835.

34.Old Parochial Registers of Scotland, Edinburgh, Midlothian, Scotland, St. Cuthbert's Church, Marriages (includes index), 1833-1841, FHL Microfilm Roll 1066765, Item 2, contains the marriage record of Adam Edwards and Isabella Scott, daughter of William Scott, farm servant in Peebles, dated December 28, 1838.

35.Old Parochial Registers of Scotland, Edinburgh, Midlothian, Scotland, St. Cuthbert's Church, Baptisms, 1793-1817, FHL Microfilm Roll 1066755 contains the baptismal records of Alexander, Robert, and George Edwards. Also Old Parochial Registers of Scotland, Edinburgh, Midlothian, Scotland, St. Cuthbert's Church, Baptisms, 1817-1819, FHL Microfilm Roll 1066756 contains the baptismal record of Susan Edwards. Also Old Parochial Registers of Scotland, Edinburgh, Midlothian, Scotland, St. Cuthbert's Church, Baptisms (includes index), 1820-1826, FHL Microfilm Roll 0993529 contains the baptismal records of Adam and Jane Edwards.

36.Old Parochial Registers of Scotland, Edinburgh, Midlothian, Scotland, St. Cuthbert's Church, Baptisms (includes index), 1833-1843, FHL Microfilm Roll 0103061 contains the baptismal record of George Edwards born September 24, 1839.

37.Old Parochial Registers of Scotland, Edinburgh, Midlothian, Scotland, St. Cuthbert's Church, Baptisms (includes index), 1833-1843, FHL Microfilm Roll 0103061 contains the baptismal record of Ann Edwards born May 9, 1837 and George Edwards born February 21, 1940.

38.Old Parochial Registers of Scotland, Edinburgh, Midlothian, Scotland, St. Cuthbert's Church, Baptisms (includes index), 1843-1854, FHL Microfilm Roll 0103062, contains no record of the Edwards children's baptisms.

39.Keay and Keay, 230, 399. Also, Baptisms, Free Church of Scotland, 1843 to 1900 (Dean, Edinburgh, Chalmers), Edinburgh, Midlothian, FHL Microfiche 6901840, contains no record of the Edwards children's baptisms.

40.No records of the United Presbyterian Church of Scotland were examined for the baptism of any of the Edwards children.

41.William Edwards, Civil War Pension Application, SO 52835, SC 34984, Records of the Veterans Administration, Record Group 15, National Archives, Washington, D.C., deposition of Annie Adam (Edwards) Chambers.

42.Old Parochial Registers of Scotland, Dundee, Angus, Parish Church of Dundee, Marriages, v. 13, 1783-1803; Marriages, v. 14, 1804-1819, FHL Microfilm Roll 0993401. After the Banns Matrimonial were read at St. Cuthbert's Kirk in Edinburgh on May 17, 1806, for George Edwards and Agnes Adam, daughter of John Adam resident of Dundee, the couple was married on May 21, 1806, at the Parish Church of Dundee.

43.Lewis, Volume I:386.

44.Rev. John Marius Wilson, *The Imperial Gazetteer of Scotland; or Dictionary of Scottish Topography, Compiled From the Most Recent Authorities, and Forming a Complete Body of Scottish Geography, Phyal, Statistical, and Historical*, (London and Edinburgh: A. Fullarton & Company, c. 1861), Volume I:515.

45.William Edwards, Civil War Pension Application, SO 52835, SC 34984, Records of the Veterans Administration, Record Group 15, National Archives, Washington, D.C. The extract of Adam Edwards' marriage certificate states he lived at # 3 Warriston *Crescent* (sic).

46.1841 Scotland Census, Midlothian, Edinburgh St Cuthbert's Parish; ED 20A; page 7; line 1250, <<www.ancestry.com>>, downloaded January 29, 2016.

47.1841 Scotland Census, Midlothian, Edinburgh St Cuthbert's Parish; ED 20A; page 12; line 590, <<www.ancestry.com>>, downloaded January 29, 2016.

48.Wilson, Volume I:243.

49.Wilson, Volume I:519.

50.Wilson, Volume I:568,

51.William Edwards, Civil War Pension Application, SO 52835, SC 34984, Records of the Veterans Administration, Record Group 15, National Archives, Washington, D.C., deposition of Annie Adam (Edwards) Chambers.

52.This is incorrect. Adam Edwards was 18 and Isabella Scott was 20 when they were married on December 28, 1838.

53. The whereabouts of the original marriage certificate of Adam Edwards and Isabella Scott is unknown.

54. Old Parochial Registers of Scotland, Edinburgh, Midlothian, Scotland, St. Cuthbert's Church, Marriages (includes index), 1833-1841, FHL Microfilm Roll 1066765, Item 2, says Adam Edwards lived at # 3 Warriston Street (sic).

55. Old Parochial Registers of Scotland, Edinburgh, Midlothian, Scotland, St. Cuthbert's Church, Baptisms (includes index), 1833-1843, FHL Microfilm Roll 0103061 contains the baptismal record of George Edwards born September 24, 1839.

56. George Chambers and Annie A. Chambers, widow, Civil War Pension Application, SO 1304127, SC 1102701, WO 849418, WC 612527, Records of the Veterans Administration, Record Group 15, National Archives, Washington, D.C.

57. The whereabouts of the Edwards Family Bible is unknown. If it survived, it may be in the possession of the descendants of Annie Adam (Edwards) Chambers' daughter, Emma (Chambers) Spence, with whom Annie was living at the time of her death in 1927.

58. Ship Arrivals, *New York Herald - Morning Edition*, New York, New York, Monday, July 30, 1849, p. 4.

59. Entry for the Bark Mary, arrival date obscured, Target 8 (January 1, 1849 to June 30, 1852), Register of Vessels Arriving at the Port of New York from Foreign Ports, 1789-1919, National Archives Microfilm Publication M1066, Roll 6.

60. Entry for the Edwards Family, Bark Mary Passenger Manifest, July 31, 1849, p. 1, lines 1-11, Passenger List of Vessels Arriving at New York, NY, 1820-1897, National Archives Microfilm Publication M237, Roll 82.

61. William Edwards, Civil War Pension Application, SO 52835, SC 34984, Records of the Veterans Administration, Record Group 15, National Archives, Washington, D.C., deposition of Annie Adam (Edwards) Chambers.

62. Local News, *The Dollar Newspaper*, Philadelphia, Pennsylvania, Wednesday, August 7, 1850, p. 6.

63. The 1850 Philadelphia City Directory includes a listing for Gavin Watson, M.D., living at 26 S. 13th Street.

64. Philadelphia Cemetery Returns, Odd Fellows Cemetery Interments for the Week Ending August 3, 1850, Philadelphia City Archives, Philadelphia, Pennsylvania.

65. Obituary, *Philadelphia Public Ledger*, Philadelphia, Pennsylvania, Wednesday, July 31, 1850, p. 2.

66.William Edwards, Civil War Pension Application, SO 52835, SC 34984, Records of the Veterans Administration, Record Group 15, National Archives, Washington, D.C., deposition of William Scott Edwards.

67.Historic Pennsylvania Church and Town Records, Historical Society of Pennsylvania, Philadelphia, Pennsylvania, Odd Fellows Cemetery Register of Interments, HSP Microfilm Roll 1218, image 2173, <<www.ancestry.com>>, downloaded 4 October 2015 does not contain a date of death. Also, Historic Pennsylvania Church and Town Records, Historical Society of Pennsylvania, Philadelphia, Pennsylvania, Odd Fellows Cemetery Register of Interments, p. 45, HSP Microfilm Roll unknown, image 2100, <<www.ancestry.com>>, downloaded 4 October 2015 states Adam Edwards was a miller who died July 30 (sic), 1850.

68.Philadelphia Cemetery Returns, Odd Fellows Cemetery Interments for the Week Ending August 3, 1850, Philadelphia City Archives, Philadelphia, Pennsylvania.

69.1850 Mortality Schedule, Pennsylvania, Philadelphia County, City of Philadelphia, Spring Garden Ward 4, page unknown, National Archives Microfilm Publication M1838, Roll 2, line 12.

70.1850 U.S. Census (population), Pennsylvania, Philadelphia County, City of Philadelphia, Spring Garden Ward 4, page 104A, National Archives Microfilm Publication M432, Roll 819.

71.1850 U.S. Census (population), Pennsylvania, Philadelphia County, City of Philadelphia, Spring Garden Ward 4, page 113B, National Archives Microfilm Publication M432, Roll 819.

72.1850 U.S. Census (population), Pennsylvania, Philadelphia County, City of Philadelphia, North Mulberry Ward, page 464, National Archives Microfilm Publication M432, Roll 815.

73.Letter dated May 10, 1996, from Regina O'Donnell, Secretary of Lawnview Cemetery, concerning the removal of Adam Edwards to that cemetery where he was reinterred in Susquehanna Lawn, Section 55, Grave 60H.

74.Philadelphia Cemetery Returns, Philadelphia Cemetery Interments for the Week Ending January 18, 1851, Philadelphia City Archives, Philadelphia, Pennsylvania.

75.Ronaldson's Cemetery, laid out by James Ronaldson at his own expense as a public cemetery in 1827, was also known as Philadelphia Cemetery.

76.Ronaldson's Cemetery, Philadelphia, Pennsylvania, Index, Interments and Lot Books, FHL Microfilm Rolls 0382716-0382718.

77.Philadelphia Cemetery Returns, Philadelphia Cemetery Interments for the Week Ending January 18, 1851, Philadelphia City Archives, Philadelphia, Pennsylvania.

78.The 1851 Philadelphia City Directory contains a listing for Colin Arrott, M.D., living at Poplar below Schuylkill 6th (now 17th Street).

79. William Edwards, Civil War Pension Application, SO 52835, SC 34984, Records of the Veterans Administration, Record Group 15, National Archives, Washington, D.C., deposition of Annie Adam (Edwards) Chambers.

80. Helen Hutchinson Woodroofe, Compiler, *A Genealogist's Guide to Philadelphia Records - Special Publication No. 5*, (Philadelphia, Pennsylvania: Genealogical Society of Pennsylvania, 1995), 347.

81. Unsigned and undated note from Forest Hills Cemetery typed at the bottom of this author's letter to the cemetery dated August 14, 1997, in which the cemetery employee states: "The remains moved from Ronaldson (sic) are in a mass grave here at Forest Hills. We do have the books, but they are in no order. If you are ever in the area, you are more than welcome to come in an (sic) look (sic) the records yourself."

82. The 1852 Philadelphia City Directory (McElroy).

83. George Chambers and Annie A. Chambers, widow, Civil War Pension Application, SO 1304127, SC 1102701, WO 849418, WC 612527, Records of the Veterans Administration, Record Group 15, National Archives, Washington, D.C.

84. The correct spelling of Andrew Flanagan's surname is unknown.

85. The 1860 City Directory (Cohen) includes a listing for an Andrew Flannigan (sic), laborer, at 1820 Jones.

86. The 1860 City Directory (McElroy) includes a listing for an Andrew Flannagan (sic), boatman, at 1818 Jones.

87. 1860 U.S. Census (population), Pennsylvania, Philadelphia County, City of Philadelphia, 9th Ward, page 326, National Archives Microfilm Publication M653, Roll 1159.

88. In 1917, the Bureau of the Census could *not* find this entry when asked to do so by the Commissioner of Pensions. Their letter, dated April 21, 1917, is contained in the following pension file: George Chambers and Annie A. Chambers, widow, Civil War Pension Application, SO 1304127, SC 1102701, WO 849418, WC 612527, Records of the Veterans Administration, Record Group 15, National Archives, Washington, D.C. The letter reads, in part:

> You are advised that the schedules for Ward 9, (which covered the territory in which the pensioner [i.e., Annie Adam (Edwards) Chambers] claimed to have resided), Philadelphia, Philadelphia County, Pennsylvania, as returned at the Census of 1860, have been carefully examined, but we fail to find the claimant's name enumerated therein.

89. Rev. A.W. Drury, *History of the City of Dayton and Montgomery County, Ohio*, (Chicago, Illinois: The S.J. Clarke Publishing Company, 1909), 750.

90.Register - Soldiers Home Central Branch, Dayton, Ohio (1866-1938), Flanagan, Andrew, SC 206275, Reg. # 9796, Records of the United States Soldiers Home, Record Group 231, National Archives Microfilm Publication M1749, Roll 35.

91.William Edwards, Civil War Pension Application, SO 52835, SC 34,984, Records of the Veterans Administration, Record Group 15, National Archives, Washington, D.C., deposition of Annie Adam (Edwards) Chambers.

92.Obituary, *Philadelphia Public Ledger*, Philadelphia, Pennsylvania, Tuesday, July 28, 1863, p. 2.

93.1863 Death Register, City of Philadelphia, page 203, Philadelphia City Archives, Philadelphia, Pennsylvania.

94.Letter dated March 9, 1998, from Lydia M. Jones, Director, Mount Moriah Cemetery, stating that Isabella Flannigan *(sic)* is buried in Section 108, Lot 010 SE-1/4.

95.Conversation on February 21, 2000, with "Debra", Administrative Assistant, Mount Moriah Cemetery, concerning the name of the original owner of Section 108, Lot 010 SE 1/4.

96.A review of the Mount Moriah Cemetery Burial Records at the Genealogical Society of Pennsylvania, Philadelphia, Pennsylvania, on March 23, 1999, revealed that a George Edwards (30) and Lizzie Edwards (20) were buried with Isabella Flannigan (sic) in Section 108, Lot 010 SE-1/4.

97.Site visit on March 22, 1999, to Mount Moriah Cemetery, 62nd and Kingsessing Avenue, Philadelphia, Pennsylvania. Although there were no headstones on the lot where Isabella (Scott) Edwards Flanagan was buried, there was another lot in close proximity that contained several headstones reading Flannigan (sic). To date, no relationship has been established between the people named on the Flannigan (sic) headstones and Isabella (Scott) Edwards Flanagan.

98.Union Compiled Military Service Record for Andrew Flanagan, Co. K, 99th Pennsylvania Volunteer Infantry, Records of the Adjutant General's Office, Record Group 94, National Archives, Washington, D.C.

99.His death record states that he was born in Philadelphia.

100.Frank Hamilton Taylor, *Philadelphia in the Civil War 1861-1865*, (Philadelphia, Pennsylvania: Dunlop Printing Company, 1913), 118.

101.Taylor, 214.

102.Entry for Andrew Falligan (sic), Volume I, p. 6, # 245, Pennsylvania Soldiers and Sailors Home Records, 1864 - 1883, Pennsylvania State Archives, Harrisburg, Pennsylvania, Microfilm Roll 492.

103. 1870 U.S. Census (population), Second Enumeration, Pennsylvania, Philadelphia County, City of Philadelphia, 8th Ward, page 117B, National Archives Publication M593, Roll 1421.

104. 1880 U.S. Census (population), Ohio, Montgomery County, E.D. 169, pages 585 - 620, National Archives Microfilm Publication T9, Roll 1052.

105. Register - Soldiers Home Central Branch, Dayton, Ohio (1866-1938), Flanagan, Andrew, SC 206275, Reg. # 9796, Records of the United States Soldiers Home, Record Group 231, National Archives Microfilm Publication M1749, Roll 35.

106. Andrew Flanigan (sic), Civil War Pension Application, SO 198080, SC 206275, Records of the Veterans Administration, Record Group 15, National Archives, Washington, D.C.

107. *List of Pensioners on the Roll January 1, 1883*, 5 volumes (Baltimore, Maryland: Genealogical Publishing Company, 1970), Volume III:248.

108. Philadelphia Cemetery Returns, Mount Moriah Cemetery Interments for the Week Ending May 20, 1882, Philadelphia City Archives, Philadelphia, Pennsylvania.

109. News Story, *Philadelphia Inquirer*, Philadelphia, Pennsylvania, Wednesday, May 17, 1882, p. 3, says:

> Anna M. Ross Post, No. 94, G.A.R., has taken charge of and interred in their
> (sic) lot, at Mount Moriah Cemetery, Andrew Flanagan, an inmate of the
> National Home, at Dayton, Ohio, who died while on a visit to this city.

110. A review of the Mount Moriah Cemetery Burial Records at the Genealogical Society of Pennsylvania, Philadelphia, Pennsylvania, on March 23, 1999, revealed that Andrew Flanagan was buried March 15, 1882, in Section 133, Lot 115.

111. Find-A-Grave Memorial # 34301690, Pvt. Andrew Flanigan, (no headstone photograph), added February 28, 2009, Mount Moriah Cemetery, Philadelphia, Philadelphia County, Pennsylvania, <<www.findagrave.com>>, says Section 133, Lot 115, Grave 58.

112. Scharf and Westcott, *History of Philadelphia: 1609-1884*, 3 volumes (Philadelphia, Pennsylvania: Everts and Company, 1884), 1787.

113. Philadelphia Soldiers' Home Records, 1866-1883, FHL Microfilm Roll 1032842, items 4-6.

114. Register - Soldiers Home Central Branch, Dayton, Ohio (1866-1938), Flanagan, Andrew, SC 206275, Reg. # 9796, Records of the United States Soldiers Home, Record Group 231, National Archives Microfilm Publication M1749, Roll 35.

115. Petition for Naturalization of George Edwards, Court of Common Pleas for the City and County of Philadelphia, October 25, 1860, Philadelphia City Archives, Philadelphia, Pennsylvania.

116.A review of the Mount Moriah Cemetery Burial Records at the Genealogical Society of Pennsylvania, Philadelphia, Pennsylvania, on March 23, 1999, revealed that a George Leacock was buried on August 8, 1872, in Section 108, Lot 010 SE-1/4, with Isabella Flannigan (sic), George Edwards, and Lizzie Edwards. The relationship of George Leacock to the Edwards family is unknown.

117.Obituary, *Philadelphia Public Ledger*, Philadelphia, Pennsylvania, Friday, March 12, 1869, p. 2, and Saturday, March 13, 1869, p. 2.

118.Letter dated September 1, 1999, from F.F. Daniel J. Kenney, Archivist, Historian, Fireman's Hall, 147 North 2nd Street, Philadelphia, Pennsylvania 19106-2010.

119.Scharf and Westcott, 1910.

120.Scharf and Westcott, 1912.

121.Return of Marriages, 1864, Fourth Quarter to 1865, Third Quarter (Rev. M.C. Suthlieu), City of Philadelphia, Pennsylvania, FHL Microfilm Roll 1765115.

122.Church of the Redemption (Protestant Episcopal) Marriage Register (1855-1875), Genealogical Society of Pennsylvania, Philadelphia, Pennsylvania, Microfilm Roll XCh/169.

123.Obituary, *Philadelphia Public Ledger*, Philadelphia, Pennsylvania, Friday, March 12, 1869, p. 2, and Saturday, March 13, 1869, p. 2.

124.Scharf and Westcott, 2078.

125.Albert C. Stevens, *The Cyclopedia of Fraternities - A Compilation of Existing Authentic Information and the Results of Original Investigations as to the Origin, Derivation, Founders, Development Aims, Emblems, Character, and Personnel of More than Six Hundred Secret Societies in the United States* (New York: Hamilton Printing and Publishing Company, 1899), 299.

126.Obituary, *Philadelphia Public Ledger*, Philadelphia, Pennsylvania, Friday, March 12, 1869, p. 2, and Saturday, March 13, 1869, p. 2.

127.A review of the Mount Moriah Cemetery Burial Records at the Genealogical Society of Pennsylvania, Philadelphia, Pennsylvania, on April 16, 1997, revealed that George Edwards was buried in Section 108, Lot 010 SE-1/4. His mother was buried in the same plot in 1863.

128.Conversation on February 21, 2000, with "Debra," Administrative Assistant, Mount Moriah Cemetery, concerning the name of the original owner of Section 108, Lot 010 SE-1/4.

129.Bond of Administration in the Matter of the Estate of George Edwards, Administration No. 199, Year 1869, dated March 23, 1869, Register of Wills, Orphans Court, Philadelphia County, Philadelphia, Pennsylvania.

130. 1870 U.S. Census (population), First Enumeration, Pennsylvania, Philadelphia County, City of Philadelphia, 15th Ward, page 514B, National Archives Microfilm Publication M593, Roll 1399.

131. 1870 U.S. Census (population), Second Enumeration, Pennsylvania, Philadelphia County, City of Philadelphia, 15th Ward, page 429B, National Archives Microfilm Publication M593, Roll 1428.

132. William Edwards, Civil War Pension Application, SO 52835, SC 34984, Records of the Veterans Administration, Record Group 15, National Archives, Washington, D.C., deposition of Annie Adam (Edwards) Chambers.

133. 1860 U.S. Census (population), Pennsylvania, Philadelphia County, City of Philadelphia, 9th Ward, page 326, National Archives Microfilm Publication M653, Roll 1159.

134. In the 1860 census, the ages of Isabella (Scott) Edwards Flanagan and her three children are all reported incorrectly. Isabella may have been attempting to conceal the fact that she was about 12 years older than Andrew Flanagan, her second husband, or someone else in the family or possibly a neighbor may have made an erroneous report to the census taker.

135. Union Compiled Military Service Record for Robert Edwards, Co. C, 109th Pennsylvania Volunteer Infantry, Records of the Adjutant General's Office, Record Group 94, National Archives, Washington, D.C.

136. The 109th Regiment was assigned to Prince's Brigade.

137. Samuel P. Bates, *History of the Pennsylvania Volunteers 1861-1865*, 5 volumes, (Harrisburg, Pennsylvania: State Printer, 1869), 954.

138. Records of Movements and Activities of Volunteer Union Organizations, 109th Regiment, Pennsylvania Volunteer Infantry, Company C, National Archives Microfilm Publication M594, Roll 179.

139. Edward J. Stackpole, *From Cedar Mountain to Antietam*. (Harrisburg, Pennsylvania: Stackpole Books, 1993), 338.

140. *The War of the Rebellion - A Compilation of the Official Records of the Union and Confederate Armies*, (Washington, D.C.: Government Printing Office, 1887), Series I, Volume XIX, Part II, p 584.

141. Union Compiled Military Service Record for Robert Edwards, Co. F, 156th Pennsylvania Volunteer Infantry, Records of the Adjutant General's Office, Record Group 94, National Archives, Washington, D.C.

142. This notation probably refers to Lieutenant Colonel Charles Ernenwein, an officer in the 21st Regiment PA Infantry, a three month organization that completed its term on August 9, 1861.

143. The Captain Farran who enlisted Robert Edwards in the 156th Regiment appears to have been the same man who was Robert Edwards' commanding officer in the 109th Regiment and who resigned his commission in that Regiment with the following mystifying letter to his commanding officer that is contained in his compiled military service record:

Camp of 109th Regt. Penn. Vol.
Bolivar Hights (sic) Va. Nov. 3rd 1862

Brig. Genl. S. Williams
Asst. Adjt. Genl. Army of the Potomac
Sir:
    Feeling my incompetency for the proper discharge of the military duties devolving upon me, I respectfully tender this resignation as Captain of Co. C 109th Regt P.V.

Very resptly your obt servant
Joseph P. Farran

    According to Captain Farran's records, his resignation was accepted on November 14, 1862, by Major General Burnside. He must have returned immediately to Philadelphia (possibly on the same train as Robert Edwards) where he joined Colonel Ernenwein in recruiting men for the 156th Regiment.

144. News Story, *Philadelphia Public Ledger*, Tuesday, November 4, 1862, p. 1.

145. Samuel P. Bates, *History of the Pennsylvania Volunteers - 1861 - 1865*. (Harrisburg, Pennsylvania: State Printer, 1869), Volume IV:105.

146. 1870 U.S. Census (population), First Enumeration, Pennsylvania, Philadelphia County, City of Philadelphia, 9th Ward, page 129, National Archives Microfilm Publication M593, Roll 1394.

147. Return of Marriages, 1863 to 1864, First Quarter (Pastor M.D. Kourtz), City of Philadelphia, Pennsylvania, FHL Microfilm Roll 1765018.

148. Church of the Redemption (Protestant Episcopal) Marriage Register (1855-1875), Genealogical Society of Pennsylvania, Philadelphia, Pennsylvania, Microfilm Roll XCh/169.

149. 1865 Death Register, City of Philadelphia, page 261, Philadelphia City Archives, Philadelphia, Pennsylvania.

150. This and That Diseases, Medical Terms, Epidemics, Copyright © 1998 by Shirley Hornbeck, <<http://homepages.rootsweb.ancestry.com/~hornbeck/disease.htm>>, downloaded 15 November 2015.

151. A review of the Mount Moriah Cemetery Burial Records at the Genealogical Society of Pennsylvania, Philadelphia, Pennsylvania, on April 16, 1997, revealed that Lizzie Edwards was buried in Section 108, Lot 10 SE-1/4.

152. Return of Marriages, 1867, Fourth Quarter (T.A. Fernley) to 1868, Fourth Quarter (Rev. John Kuntz), City of Philadelphia, Pennsylvania, FHL Microfilm Roll 1765118.

153. Church of the Redemption (Protestant Episcopal) Marriage Register (1855-1875), Genealogical Society of Pennsylvania, Philadelphia, Pennsylvania, Microfilm Roll XCh/169.

154. 1870 U.S. Census (population), First Enumeration, Pennsylvania, Philadelphia County, City of Philadelphia, 9th Ward, page 129, National Archives Microfilm Publication M593, Roll 1394.

155. 1870 U.S. Census (population), Second Enumeration, Pennsylvania, Philadelphia County, City of Philadelphia, 15th Ward, page 550A, National Archives Microfilm Publication M593, Roll 1428.

156. Philadelphia, Pennsylvania, Death Certificates, 1803-1915, Burials at Cathedral Cemetery Through Saturday, July 2, 1870, FHL Microfilm Roll 1994771. NOTE: St. Joseph's Hospital was located on the south side of Girard Avenue between 16th & 17th Streets.

157. Obituary, *Philadelphia Pubic Ledger*, Saturday, June 25, 1870, p. 2 says:

> McFEELY - On the 24th instant, ROSA (sic) McFEELY, aged 22 years. The relatives and friends of the family are respectfully invited to attend the funeral from St. Joseph's Hospital this (Saturday) afternoon, at 3 o'clock. Interment at Cathedral Cemetery.

158. Pennsylvania and New Jersey, Church and Town Records, 1708-1985, Historical Society of Pennsylvania, Old Cathedral Catholic Cemetery, Rose McFeely, buried June 25, 1870, Section B, Range 4, Lot No. 23, 2nd from East.

159. Philadelphia, Pennsylvania, Death Certificates, 1803-1915, Burials at Cathedral Cemetery Through Saturday, June 25, 1870, FHL Microfilm Roll 1994771.

160. Pennsylvania and New Jersey, Church and Town Records, 1708-1985, Historical Society of Pennsylvania, Old Cathedral Catholic Cemetery, Rose McFeely, buried June 20, 1870, "Free Grave."

161. William Edwards, Civil War Pension Application, SO 52835, SC 34984, Records of the Veterans Administration, Record Group 15, National Archives, Washington, D.C.

162. 1880 U.S. Census (population), Pennsylvania, Philadelphia County, City of Philadelphia, E.D. 126, sheet 20, line 1, National Archives Microfilm Publication T9, Roll 1170.

163. The record of the marriage of Robert Edwards and Mary Dougherty could not be located in any of the following microfilm publications: Returns of Marriages, 1872, Fourth Quarter to 1873, Third Quarter (John B. Buck), City of Philadelphia, Pennsylvania, FHL Microfilm Roll 1765164. Also, Returns of Marriage, 1873, Third Quarter (Rev. Robert Adair) to 1874, Second Quarter (M.H. Sisty), City of Philadelphia, Pennsylvania, FHL Microfilm Roll 1769059. Also,

Returns of Marriage, 1874, Second Quarter (M.H. Sisty continued) to 1875, Second Quarter (Rev. William Major), City of Philadelphia, Pennsylvania, FHL Microfilm Roll 1769060. Also, Returns of Marriages, 1875, Second Quarter (Rev. William Major) to 1876, Second Quarter (Rev. Jesse Yeakel), City of Philadelphia, Pennsylvania, FHL Microfilm Roll 1769061. Also, Returns of Marriages, 1876, Second Quarter (F. Wroohan) to 1877, Second Quarter (Rev. C. Niel), City of Philadelphia, Pennsylvania, FHL Microfilm Roll 1769062.

164. Union Compiled Military Service Record for Robert Edwards, Co. C, 109th Pennsylvania Volunteer Infantry, Records of the Adjutant General's Office, Record Group 94, National Archives, Washington, D.C.

165. Return of Marriages, 1867, Fourth Quarter (T.A. Fernley) to 1868, Fourth Quarter (Rev. John Kuntz), City of Philadelphia, Pennsylvania, FHL Microfilm Roll 1765118.

166. 1870 U.S. Census (population), First Enumeration, Pennsylvania, Philadelphia County, City of Philadelphia, 9th Ward, page 129, National Archives Microfilm Publication M593, Roll 1394.

167. 1880 U.S. Census (population), Pennsylvania, Philadelphia County, City of Philadelphia, E.D. 126, sheet 20, line 1, National Archives Microfilm Publication T9, Roll 1170.

168. Obituary, *Philadelphia Public Ledger*, Saturday, May 21, 1881, p. 2.

169. 1881 Death Register, City of Philadelphia, page 208, Philadelphia City Archives, Philadelphia, Pennsylvania.

170. Trinity Memorial Church, Philadelphia, Pennsylvania: Episcopal: 22nd and Spruce St., Parishioners -- Baptisms 1858-1892, 1891-1911 -- Confirmations 1859-1891, 1891-1910 -- Communicants -- Marriages 1858-1892, 1891-1910 -- Burials 1858-1891, 1891-1911 -- Offerings -- List of families -- Index, FHL Microfilm Roll 1723673, Item 2.

171. A review of the Mount Moriah Cemetery Burial Records at the Genealogical Society of Pennsylvania, Philadelphia, Pennsylvania, on April 16, 1997, revealed that Robert Edwards was buried in Section 204, Lot 503, a plot belonging to his brother-in-law, George Chambers.

172. Union Compiled Military Service Record for William Edwards, Co. D, 23rd Pennsylvania Volunteer Infantry, Records of the Adjutant General's Office, Record Group 94, National Archives, Washington, D.C.

173. Scharf and Westcott, 817.

174. 1860 U.S. Census (population), Pennsylvania, Philadelphia County, City of Philadelphia, 9th Ward, page 326, National Archives Microfilm Publication M653, Roll 1159.

175. Frederick A. Dyer, *A Compendium of the War of the Rebellion*. (New York and London: Thomas Yoseloff, 1959), Volume III:1584, 1585.

176. Samuel P. Bates, *History of the Pennsylvania Volunteers - 1861-1865*. (Harrisburg, Pennsylvania: State Printer, 1869), Volume I:308-316.

177. Union Compiled Military Service Record for William Edwards, Co. D, 23rd Pennsylvania Volunteer Infantry, Records of the Adjutant General's Office, Record Group 94, National Archives, Washington, D.C.

178. William Edwards, Civil War Pension Application, SO 52835, SC 34984, Records of the Veterans Administration, Record Group 15, National Archives, Washington, D.C.

179. Union Compiled Military Service Record for William Edwards, Co. D, 23rd Pennsylvania Volunteer Infantry, Records of the Adjutant General's Office, Record Group 94, National Archives, Washington, D.C.

180. William Edwards, Civil War Pension Application, SO 52835, SC 34984, Records of the Veterans Administration, Record Group 15, National Archives, Washington, D.C.

181. Union Compiled Military Service Record for William Edwards, Co. D, 23rd Pennsylvania Volunteer Infantry, Records of the Adjutant General's Office, Record Group 94, National Archives, Washington, D.C.

182. Petition for Naturalization of William Edwards, District Court for the City and County of Philadelphia, September 30, 1864, Philadelphia City Archives, Philadelphia, Pennsylvania.

183. William Edwards, Civil War Pension Application, SO 52835, SC 34984, Records of the Veterans Administration, Record Group 15, National Archives, Washington, D.C.

184. List of Pensioners on the Roll January 1, 1883, 5 volumes (Baltimore: Genealogical Publishing Company, 1970), Volume II:764.

185. William Edwards, Civil War Pension Application, SO 52835, SC 34984, Records of the Veterans Administration, Record Group 15, National Archives, Washington, D.C.

186. William Edwards, Civil War Pension Application, SO 52835, SC 34984, Records of the Veterans Administration, Record Group 15, National Archives, Washington, D.C.

187. Porter, a dark-brown beer resembling light stout, made from charred or browned malt.

188. George Chambers and Annie A. Chambers, widow, Civil War Pension Application, SO 1304127, SC 1102701, WO 849418, WC 612527, Records of the Veterans Administration, Record Group 15, National Archives, Washington, D.C.

189. 1870 U.S. Census (population), First Enumeration, Pennsylvania, Philadelphia County, City of Philadelphia, 8th Ward, page 169, National Archives Microfilm Publication M593, Roll 1393.

190. 1870 U.S. Census (population), Second Enumeration, Pennsylvania, Philadelphia County, City of Philadelphia, 8th Ward, page 117B, National Archives Microfilm Publication M593, Roll 1421.

191. 1900 U.S. Census (population), Pennsylvania, Philadelphia County, City of Philadelphia, E.D. 140, sheet 3, line 58, National Archives Microfilm Publication T623, Roll 1455.

192. 1910 U.S. Census (population), Pennsylvania, Philadelphia County, City of Philadelphia, E.D. 112, Family Number 130, National Archives Microfilm Publication T624, Roll 1389.

193. Philadelphia Cemetery Returns, Cathedral Cemetery Interments for the Week Ending October 18, 1873, Philadelphia City Archives, Philadelphia, Pennsylvania.

194. Obituary, *Philadelphia Public Ledger*, Monday, October 13, 1873, p. 2.

195. Letter dated April 9, 1999, from the Archdiocese of Philadelphia, Secretariat for Temporal Services, 111 South 28th Street, Philadelphia, Pennsylvania 19104 providing a profile of the burials in the plot (Section U, Range 2, Lot 34) owned by William J. Martin in Old Cathedral Cemetery.

196. Letter dated May 18, 2001, from the Philadelphia Archdiocesan Historical Research Center, 100 East Wynnewood Road, Wynnewood, Pennsylvania 19096-3001 provides the date William Edwards and Rose Clark were married, the date of William Edwards' conversion, and the date of birth and baptism of each of their nine children.

197. William Edwards, Civil War Pension Application, SO 52835, SC 34984, Records of the Veterans Administration, Record Group 15, National Archives, Washington, D.C., contains a report prepared by a Special Examiner in 1910 that says William Scott Edwards married his second wife, Rose Clark, who was a Roman Catholic, on August 20 (sic), 1875. Reportedly, the marriage was solemnized by Father Riley (sic).

198. The record of the marriage of William Edwards and Rose Clark could not be located in the following microfilm publications: Returns of Marriage, 1874, Second Quarter (M.H. Sisty continued) to 1875, Second Quarter (Rev. William Major), City of Philadelphia, Pennsylvania, FHL Microfilm Roll 1769060. Also, Returns of Marriages, 1875, Second Quarter (Rev. William Major) to 1876, Second Quarter (Rev. Jesse Yeakel), City of Philadelphia, Pennsylvania, FHL Microfilm Roll 1769061.

199. Letter dated May 18, 2001, from the Philadelphia Archdiocesan Historical Research Center, 100 East Wynnewood Road, Wynnewood, Pennsylvania 19096-3001 provides the date William Edwards and Rose Clark were married, the date of William Edwards' conversion, and the date of birth and baptism of each of their nine children.

200. 1880 U.S. Census (population), Pennsylvania, Philadelphia County, City of Philadelphia, E.D. 137, sheet 7, line 7, National Archives Microfilm Publication T9, Roll 1171.

201. 1890 U.S. Census (special schedule - Union veterans and widows), Pennsylvania, Philadelphia County, City of Philadelphia, E.D. 148, National Archives Microfilm Publication M123, Roll 78.

202. 1900 U.S. Census (population), Pennsylvania, Philadelphia County, City of Philadelphia, E.D. 140, sheet 3, line 58, National Archives Microfilm Publication T623, Roll 1455.

203. 1910 U.S. Census (population), Pennsylvania, Philadelphia County, City of Philadelphia, E.D. 112, Family Number 130, National Archives Microfilm Publication T624, Roll 1389.

204. Letter dated December 23, 1997, from the Archdiocese of Philadelphia, Secretariat for Temporal Services, 111 South 28th Street, Philadelphia, Pennsylvania 19104 providing a profile of the burials in the plot (Section B, Range 4, Lot 26) owned by John Clark in Old Cathedral Cemetery.

205. Letter dated May 18, 2001, from the Philadelphia Archdiocesan Historical Research Center, 100 East Wynnewood Road, Wynnewood, Pennsylvania 19096-3001 provides the date William Edwards and Rose Clark were married, the date of William Edwards' conversion, and the date of birth and baptism of each of their nine children.

206. Letter dated May 3, 1999, from Margaret Atkinson, Secretary, Grand Army of the Republic Civil War Museum and Library, Ruan House, 4278 Griscom Street, Philadelphia, Pennsylvania 19124 transmitting a Personal War Sketch of William Scott Edwards prepared on February 11, 1898, along with information concerning his date of death and burial location.

207. Scharf and Westcott, 2076.

208. Death Certificate for Rose Edwards, February 15, 1907, # 4827 & # 18744, Pennsylvania Division of Vital Statistics, New Castle, Pennsylvania 16103.

209. Obituary, *Philadelphia Public Ledger*, Saturday, February 16, 1907, p. 9 and Sunday, February 17, 1907.

210. Letter dated December 23, 1997, from the Archdiocese of Philadelphia, Secretariat for Temporal Services, 111 South 28th Street, Philadelphia, Pennsylvania 19104 providing a profile of the burials in the plot (Section B, Range 4, Lot 26) owned by John Clark in Old Cathedral Cemetery.

211. Death Certificate for William Edwards, January 7, 1911, # 5699 & # 686, Pennsylvania Division of Vital Statistics, New Castle, Pennsylvania 16103.

212. Obituary, *Philadelphia Public Ledger*, Sunday, January 8, 1911, p. 9.

213. Veterans Administration Pension Payment Cards, 1907-1933, William Edwards, SC 34984, National Archives Microfilm Publication Number M850, Roll 664.

214. William Edwards, Civil War Pension Application, SO 52835, SC 34984, Records of the Veterans Administration, Record Group 15, National Archives, Washington, D.C.

215. Letter dated December 23, 1997, from the Archdiocese of Philadelphia, Secretariat for Temporal Services, 111 South 28th Street, Philadelphia, Pennsylvania 19104 providing a profile of the burials in the plot (Section B, Range 4, Lot 26) owned by John Clark in Old Cathedral Cemetery.

216. Conversation on April 25, 1996, and November 29, 1996, with Josephine Thompson Marshall, 121 Reillywood Avenue, Haddonfield, New Jersey 08033.

217. For complete information on the Chambers family, see the Chambers Family History.

218. Church of the Redemption (Protestant Episcopal) Marriage Register (1855-1875), Historical Society of Pennsylvania, Philadelphia, Pennsylvania, Microfilm Roll XCh/169.

219. 1866 Marriage Register, City of Philadelphia, page 77, Philadelphia City Archives, Philadelphia, Pennsylvania.

220. Scharf and Westcott, 828.

221. George Chambers and Annie A. Chambers, widow, Civil War Pension Application, SO 1304127, SC 1102701, WO 849418, WC 612527, Records of the Veterans Administration, Record Group 15, National Archives, Washington, D.C.

222. 1850 U.S. Census (population), Pennsylvania, Philadelphia County, City of Philadelphia, Spring Garden Ward 4, page 104A, National Archives Microfilm Publication M432, Roll 819.

223. 1850 U.S. Census (population), Pennsylvania, Philadelphia County, City of Philadelphia, North Mulberry Ward, page 464, National Archives Microfilm Publication, M432, Roll 815.

224. George Chambers and Annie A. Chambers, widow, Civil War Pension Application, SO 1304127, SC 1102701, WO 849418, WC 612527, Records of the Veterans Administration, Record Group 15, National Archives, Washington, D.C.

225. Death Certificate for Thomas John Clark, January 25, 1949, # 7302 & # 1942, Pennsylvania Division of Vital Statistics, New Castle, Pennsylvania, 16103 states that his father was John Clark and his mother's maiden name was Emma Chambers.

226. John Clark's sister, Rose Clark, married William Scott Edwards (Annie's brother) in 1875 making for a very neat circle of in-laws and first cousins.

227. Church of the Redemption (Protestant Episcopal) Baptismal Register, Historical Society of Pennsylvania, Philadelphia, Pennsylvania, Microfilm Roll XCh/169.

228. Church of the Redemption (Protestant Episcopal) Baptismal Register, Historical Society of Pennsylvania, Philadelphia, Pennsylvania, Microfilm Roll XCh/169.

229. Church of the Redemption (Protestant Episcopal) Baptismal Register, Historical Society of Pennsylvania, Philadelphia, Pennsylvania, Microfilm Roll XCh/169.

230. 1870 U.S. Census (population), First Enumeration, Pennsylvania, Philadelphia County, City of Philadelphia, 10th Ward, page 417, National Archives Microfilm Publication M593, Roll 1395.

231. 1870 U.S. Census (population), Second Enumeration, Pennsylvania, Philadelphia County, City of Philadelphia, 10th Ward, page 34B, National Archives Microfilm Publication M593, Roll 1423.

232. Obituary, *Philadelphia Public Ledger*, Monday, November 20, 1871, p. 2 and Tuesday, November 21, 1871, p. 2.

233. Letter dated July 20, 1995, from Lydia M. Jones, Director, Mount Moriah Cemetery, concerning the plot owned by George W. Chambers (Section 204, Lot 503).

234. The 1879 Philadelphia City Directory.

235. 1880 U.S. Census (population), Pennsylvania, Philadelphia County, City of Philadelphia, E.D. 164, sheet 16, line 22, National Archives Microfilm Publication T9, Roll 1171.

236. Conversation on April 25, 1996, and November 29, 1996, with Josephine Thompson Marshall, 121 Reillywood Avenue, Haddonfield, New Jersey 08033.

237. George Chambers and Annie A. Chambers, widow, Civil War Pension Application, SO 1304127, SC 1102701, WO 849418, WC 612527, Records of the Veterans Administration, Record Group 15, National Archives, Washington, D.C.

238. George Chambers and Annie A. Chambers, widow, Civil War Pension Application, SO 1304127, SC 1102701, WO 849418, WC 612527, Records of the Veterans Administration, Record Group 15, National Archives, Washington, D.C.

239. George Chambers and Annie A. Chambers, widow, Civil War Pension Application, SO 1304127, SC 1102701, WO 849418, WC 612527, Records of the Veterans Administration, Record Group 15, National Archives, Washington, D.C.

240. The 1889 Philadelphia City Directory.

241. The 1897 Philadelphia City Directory. NOTE: The 1897 City Directory says 3233 Marston for George Chambers and 3223 Marston for William Chambers.

242. Letter dated July 20, 1995, from Lydia M. Jones, Director, Mount Moriah Cemetery, concerning the plot owned by George W. Chambers (Section 204, Lot 503).

243. William Edwards, Civil War Pension Application, SO 52835, SC 34984, Records of the Veterans Administration, Record Group 15, National Archives, Washington, D.C.

244. George Chambers and Annie A. Chambers, widow, Civil War Pension Application, SO 1304127, SC 1102701, WO 849418, WC 612527, Records of the Veterans Administration, Record Group 15, National Archives, Washington, D.C.

245. Death Certificate for George W. Chambers, May 9, 1906, # 12476 & # 49558, Pennsylvania Division of Vital Statistics, New Castle, Pennsylvania 16103.

246. George Chambers and Annie A. Chambers, widow, Civil War Pension Application, SO 1304127, SC 1102701, WO 849418, WC 612527, Records of the Veterans Administration, Record Group 15, National Archives, Washington, D.C.

247. Veterans Administration Pension Payment Cards, 1907-1933, Annie A. Chambers, WC 612527, National Archives Microfilm Publication Number M850, Roll 376.

248. Conversation on April 25, 1996, and November 29, 1996, with Josephine Thompson Marshall, 121 Reillywood Avenue, Haddonfield, New Jersey 08033.

249. Death Certificate for Annie A. Chambers, December 27, 1927, # 110928 & # 26098, Pennsylvania Division of Vital Statistics, New Castle, Pennsylvania 16103.

250. Conversation on July 31, 1995, with William Scott Chambers, 325 N.W. 95th Avenue, Plantation, Florida 33324. He could not recall for certain, but he believed that the funeral was held from the home of William and Emma (Chambers) Spence at 7119 Upland Street in West Philadelphia.

251. Letter dated July 20, 1995, from Lydia M. Jones, Director, Mount Moriah Cemetery, concerning the plot owned by George W. Chambers (Section 204, Lot 503).

Possible
Pedigree Chart for
Adam Edwards

Adam Edwards

b: 22 Oct 1820 in Edinburgh, Midlothian, Scotland
m: 28 Dec 1838 in Edinburgh, Midlothian, Scotland
d: 30 Jul 1850 in Philadelphia, Pennsylvania

George Edwards

b: Abt. 1786
m: 21 May 1806 in Dundee, Angus, Scotland
d:

Name:

b:
m:
d:

Name:

b:
m:
d:

Name:

b:
d:

Name:

b:
d:

Agnes Adam

b: Abt. 1786 in Monikie, Angus, Scotland
d:

John Adam

b: Bef. 01 Dec 1745 in Monifieth, Angus, Scotland
m: 11 Nov 1775 in Drumstrudy Muir, Monifieth, Angus, Scotland
d: Aft. 1818 in Dundee, Angus, Scotland

Jean Edward

b: Bef. 20 Jan 1745 in Monikie, Angus, Scotland
d:

John Adam

b: Bef. 14 May 1710 in Montrose,...
m: 24 Oct 1741 in Farnell, Angus,...
d: Aft. 1775 in Monifieth, Angus,...

Anna Buchan

b: Bef. 06 Jan 1711 in Farnell, Angus, Scotland
d: 17 Jun 1775 in Monifieth, Angus, Scotland

David Edward

b:
m:
d:

Margaret Brechim

b:
d:

Name:

b:
m:
d:

Name:

b:
d:

Possible
Pedigree Chart for
Isabella Scott

William Scott

b: 17 May 1786 in Selkirk, County
Selkirk, Scotland
m: 15 Jun 1810 in Selkirk, County
Selkirk, Scotland
d: Aft. 1840

Andrew Scott

b:
m:
d:

Name:

b:
m:
d:

Name:

b:
d:

Margaret Hopkirk

b:
d:

Name:

b:
m:
d:

Name:

b:
d:

Isabella Scott

b: 07 Jun 1818 in Galashiels,
County Selkirk, Scotland
m: 28 Dec 1838 in Edinburgh,
Midlothian, Scotland
d: 25 Jul 1863 in Philadelphia,
Pennsylvania

Anne Brown

b: 11 Sep 1791 in Selkirk, County
Selkirk, Scotland
d: Aft. 1840

Andrew Brown

b: 25 Mar 1762 in Selkirk, County
Selkirk, Scotland
m: 15 Mar 1787 in Selkirk, County
Selkirk, Scotland
d:

Walter Brown

b: 07 Aug 1726 in Selkirk, County...
m: 27 Apr 1750 in Selkirk, County...
d:

Janet Mitchellhill

b: Abt. 28 Mar 1726 in Robertson,
County Selkirk, Scotland
d:

Margaret Mattheson

b: Abt. 11 Oct 1769 in Ashkirk,
County Roxburgh, Scotland
d:

James Mattheson

b: Abt. 23 Mar 1729 in Minto,......
m: 01 Jul 1757 in Ashkirk, County...
d:

Anne Scott

b: Abt. 14 Jan 1728 in Hawick,
County Roxburgh, Scotland
d:

Appendix B

DEPOSITION OF ANNIE A. CHAMBERS

Case of William Edwards # 34984

On this 3rd day of June 1910 at Philadelphia, County of Philadelphia, State of Pennsylvania, before me, C.F. Barrett, a Special Examiner of the Bureau of Pensions, personally appeared Annie A. Chambers, who being by me first duly sworn to answer truly all interrogations propounded to her during this special examination of aforesaid claim for pension, deposes and says:

I am 63 years old. I am a widow and a pensioner. My husband was George Chambers, Co. D, 24th PA Volunteer Infantry. I reside at # 2823 Wharton Street, Philadelphia, Pennsylvania.

I am well acquainted with William S. Edwards. He is my only surviving brother. Our parents were Adam Edwards and Isabella Edwards. My father was English and my mother was Scotch. My father died in Philadelphia in 1850 a year after he came to this country. Mother died in 1863. My father lacked three months of being 29 years old when he died and was the father of six children. All these children were born in Scotland except one, the youngest. He was a little boy born in Philadelphia and died six months after father died. Another child died in Scotland when four years old.

With my parents came four children to this country. They are all dead, but William and me.

My parents married young, father 17 and mother 18 years old at the time.

Their first child was George not William Scott; then Robert and Adam, twins, then myself; and then the little one born here, Joseph Campbell.

My parents lived in Edinboro and all the children except the youngest was born in Edinboro. My parents were Presbyterians and the children were all baptized and christened in the Presbyterian Church when infants. I do not know in what church in Edinboro they were christened. I was not quite 16 years old when my mother died and all I know about the family history is what I used to hear mother tell. I have always had a good memory and can remember a good deal my mother told me.

Mother married in 1838. I have here in my possession mother's original marriage certificate. [Hand examiner said certificate. It is very old, creased and torn, and the ink is very faded. It is undoubtedly genuine. It reads as follows:

> At St. Cuthbert's (Cuthbert's) the twenty fourth day of December 1838.
> It is hereby certified that Adam Edward, Miller, Residing in No. 3
> Warriston Crescent Parish of St. Cuthbert's and Isabella Scott, Residing
> in Canon Street, Canonmills, Same Parish, Daughter of William Scott,
> Farm Servant in Peebles, have been three times duly and regularly
> proclaimed in order to Marriage in the Parish Church of St. Cuthberts
> and no objection offered.
>
> A.W. McFullanton, Elder
> John Adams, Session Clerk

Amount of Fee, 10s 6d

At Edinburgh the 28th day of December 1838, that Adam Edward and Isabella Scott were this day married by me is here certified.

James McFarland, Minister]

George was born first, sometime in 1839. I can't remember for certain the month, but I think it was November 1839. He was born before they had been married a year anyway.

William was the next child and was born August 17th, 1840. I am not certain as to the year, but I am as to the day of the month. I have always remembered the month and day of the month that William was born. I often heard my mother mentioned in. I also distinctly remember hearing mother say that her first two children came very quick and that her parents scolded her for having children so fast.

I feel certain that George was born in 1839 and about November; and William in August of the next year. 1840. It couldn't have been 1841 as I know mother always said he came pretty soon after George. The twins were born in September 1843; and I was born February 26, 1847.

It seems to me that mother did have a little small Bible with our births in it, but I have no idea about ever became of it. I think I had it after my mother's death, but lost all track of that Bible years ago.

DO YOU REMEMBER THE BRICKMAKERS MISSION CHURCH ON 20TH STREET ABOVE CHESTNUT STREET?

I do. It was a Methodist Mission.

I have heard you read my brother William's deposition before you. I think he is crazy. I don't think he is right bright in the brain anymore. I have noticed that his mind wanders and I have spoken to his daughter about it. He was not born in this country, nor baptized in this country. He is crazy and his health is very poor. He had to be ta–fied for dropsy a year ago.

I am not interested financially. I have had this read in full; and my answers are correctly written herein.

Signed: Annie A. Chambers

Descendants of Adam Edwards

Generation 1

1. **ADAM[1] EDWARDS** was born on 22 Oct 1820 in Edinburgh, Midlothian, Scotland. He died on 30 Jul 1850 in Philadelphia, Pennsylvania. He married Isabella Scott, daughter of William Scott and Anne Brown on 28 Dec 1838 in Edinburgh, Midlothian, Scotland. She was born on 07 Jun 1818 in Galashiels, County Selkirk, Scotland. She died on 25 Jul 1863 in Philadelphia, Pennsylvania.

    Adam Edwards and Isabella Scott had the following children:

    i. GEORGE W.[2] EDWARDS was born on 24 Sep 1839 in Edinburgh, Midlothian, Scotland. He died on 11 Mar 1869 in Philadelphia, Pennsylvania. He married Susan Brown on 27 Aug 1865 in Philadelphia, Pennsylvania. She was born in 1846 in Philadelphia, Pennsylvania.

2. ii. WILLIAM SCOTT EDWARDS was born on 17 Aug 1840 in Edinburgh, Midlothian, Scotland. He died on 07 Jan 1911 in Philadelphia, Pennsylvania. He married (1) JANE MARTIN on 04 Jul 1864. She was born about 1841 in New York. She died on 10 Oct 1873 in Philadelphia, Pennsylvania. He married (2) ROSE ANN CLARK, daughter of Thomas Clark and Ann (--?--) on 19 Aug 1875 in Philadelphia, Pennsylvania. She was born on 03 Oct 1846 in Philadelphia, Pennsylvania. She died on 15 Feb 1907 in Philadelphia, Pennsylvania.

    iii. ADAM (TWIN) EDWARDS was born in Sep 1843 in Edinburgh, Midlothian, Scotland. He died in 1847 in Edinburgh, Midlothian, Scotland.

3. iv. ROBERT HUNTER (TWIN) EDWARDS was born in Sep 1843 in Edinburgh, Midlothian, Scotland. He died on 19 May 1881 in Philadelphia, Pennsylvania. He married (1) ELIZABETH CUSACK on 05 Feb 1863 in Philadelphia, Pennsylvania. She was born about 1847 in Kentucky. She died on 09 Aug 1865 in Philadelphia, Pennsylvania. He married (2) ROSE ANN MCFEELY on 02 Feb 1868 in Philadelphia, Pennsylvania. She was born in 1847 in Ireland. She died on 24 Jun 1870 in Philadelphia, Pennsylvania. He married (3) MARY between 1872-1877. She was born about 1847 in Ireland.

4. v. ANNIE ADAM EDWARDS was born on 26 Feb 1847 in Edinburgh, Midlothian, Scotland. She died on 27 Dec 1927 in Philadelphia, Pennsylvania. She married George Washington Chambers, son of George Chambers and Elizabeth on 04 Jul 1866 in Philadelphia, Pennsylvania. He was born on 22 Feb 1841 in Philadelphia, Pennsylvania. He died on 09 May 1906 in Philadelphia, Pennsylvania.

    vi. JOSEPH CAMPBELL EDWARDS was born in Mar 1850 in Philadelphia, Pennsylvania. He died on 11 Jan 1851 in Philadelphia, Pennsylvania.

Generation 2

2. **WILLIAM SCOTT[2] EDWARDS** (Adam[1]) was born on 17 Aug 1840 in Edinburgh, Midlothian, Scotland. He died on 07 Jan 1911 in Philadelphia, Pennsylvania. He married (1) **JANE MARTIN** on 04 Jul 1864. She was born about 1841 in New York. She died on 10 Oct 1873 in Philadelphia, Pennsylvania. He married (2) **ROSE ANN CLARK**, daughter of Thomas Clark and Ann (--?--) on 19 Aug 1875 in Philadelphia, Pennsylvania. She was born on 03 Oct 1846 in Philadelphia, Pennsylvania. She died on 15 Feb 1907 in Philadelphia, Pennsylvania.

    William Scott Edwards and Rose Ann Clark had the following children:

5. i. WILLIAM SCOTT[3] EDWARDS JR. was born on 13 Jul 1876 in Philadelphia, Pennsylvania. He died on 04 Aug 1949 in Philadelphia, Pennsylvania. He married Gertrude Pierson, daughter of William Pierson and Catherine McCann on 18 Nov 1901 in Delaware. She was born on 13 Feb 1884 in Pennsylvania. She died on 23 Jun 1955 in Philadelphia, Pennsylvania.

6. ii. ROSE ANN MARIE EDWARDS was born on 20 Aug 1877 in Philadelphia, Pennsylvania. She died on 29 Jan 1946 in Philadelphia, Pennsylvania. She married James Edward Shields, son of Edward Shields and Catharine Maguire on 30 Jul 1900 in Philadelphia, Philadelphia County, Pennsylvania. He was born on 23 Aug 1876 in Philadelphia, Pennsylvania. He died on 25 Dec 1944 in Philadelphia, Pennsylvania.

7. iii. THOMAS J. EDWARDS was born on 14 Apr 1879 in Philadelphia, Pennsylvania. He died on 25 Sep 1905 in Philadelphia, Pennsylvania. He married Della M. Brown in 1902 in Philadelphia Pennsylvania. She was born on 26 Feb 1881 in Philadelphia, Pennsylvania. She died in May 1967 in Philadelphia, Pennsylvania.

iv. GEORGE EDWARDS was born on 23 Jan 1881 in Philadelphia, Pennsylvania. He died on 10 Nov 1884 in Philadelphia, Pennsylvania.

v. MARY ANN EDWARDS was born on 14 Oct 1882 in Philadelphia, Pennsylvania. She died on 09 Nov 1884 in Philadelphia, Pennsylvania.

vi. JOHN EDWARDS was born on 28 Apr 1884 in Philadelphia, Pennsylvania. He died on 30 Jun 1884 in Philadelphia, Pennsylvania.

vii. JOHN JOSEPH EDWARDS was born on 10 Jun 1885 in Philadelphia, Pennsylvania. He died on 26 Feb 1944 in Philadelphia, Pennsylvania.

viii. ISABELLA EDWARDS was born on 03 Aug 1887 in Philadelphia, Pennsylvania. She died on 24 Jul 1888 in Philadelphia, Pennsylvania.

8. ix. ISABELLA M. EDWARDS was born on 21 Sep 1889 in Philadelphia, Pennsylvania. She died about 1983. She married John A. Dougherty on 02 Jun 1907 in Philadelphia, Philadelphia County, Pennsylvania. He was born on 16 May 1886 in Philadelphia, Pennsylvania. He died between 1910-1920.

3. **ROBERT HUNTER (TWIN)[2] EDWARDS** (Adam[1]) was born in Sep 1843 in Edinburgh, Midlothian, Scotland. He died on 19 May 1881 in Philadelphia, Pennsylvania. He married (1) **ELIZABETH CUSACK** on 05 Feb 1863 in Philadelphia, Pennsylvania. She was born about 1847 in Kentucky. She died on 09 Aug 1865 in Philadelphia, Pennsylvania. He married (2) **ROSE ANN MCFEELY** on 02 Feb 1868 in Philadelphia, Pennsylvania. She was born in 1847 in Ireland. She died on 24 Jun 1870 in Philadelphia, Pennsylvania. He married (3) **MARY** between 1872-1877. She was born about 1847 in Ireland.

Robert Hunter (twin) Edwards and Rose Ann McFeely had the following child:
    i. ROSE[3] MCFEELY was born on 18 Jun 1870 in Philadelphia, Pennsylvania. She died on 19 Jun 1870 in Philadelphia, Pennsylvania.

Robert Hunter (twin) Edwards and Mary had the following child:
    ii. BELLA EDWARDS was born about 1877 in Pennsylvania.

4. **ANNIE ADAM[2] EDWARDS** (Adam[1]) was born on 26 Feb 1847 in Edinburgh, Midlothian, Scotland. She died on 27 Dec 1927 in Philadelphia, Pennsylvania. She married George Washington Chambers, son of George Chambers and Elizabeth on 04 Jul 1866 in Philadelphia, Pennsylvania. He was born on 22 Feb 1841 in Philadelphia, Pennsylvania. He died on 09 May 1906 in Philadelphia, Pennsylvania.

George Washington Chambers and Annie Adam Edwards had the following children:

9.   i.   WILLIAM SCOTT[3] CHAMBERS was born on 05 Jun 1867 in Philadelphia, Pennsylvania. He died on 05 Feb 1950 in Philadelphia, Pennsylvania. He married (1) SARAH WHITE, daughter of Richard White and Catharine (--?--) on 01 Feb 1894 in Philadelphia, Pennsylvania. She was born on 15 Oct 1868 in Philadelphia, Pennsylvania. She died on 14 Aug 1894 in Philadelphia, Pennsylvania. He married (2) JOSEPHINE IRENE REITZE, daughter of Christopher Reitze and Lucy S. Devlin on 30 Mar 1896 in Philadelphia, Pennsylvania. She was born on 04 Jul 1877 in Philadelphia, Pennsylvania. She died on 03 May 1962 in Philadelphia, Pennsylvania.

    ii.   ELIZA JANE CHAMBERS was born on 23 Oct 1869 in Philadelphia, Pennsylvania. She died on 18 Nov 1871 in Philadelphia, Pennsylvania.

10.   iii.   LYDIA E. CHAMBERS was born on 27 Feb 1872 in Philadelphia, Pennsylvania. She died on 19 Feb 1949 in Philadelphia, Pennsylvania. She married (1) LEONARD H. SMITH on 25 Aug 1909 in Philadelphia, Pennsylvania. He was born on 13 Jul 1878 in Germany. She married (2) JOHN J. ROE in 1916 in Philadelphia, Philadelphia County, Pennsylvania. He was born on 16 May 1865 in New York. He died on 15 Oct 1929 in Philadelphia, Pennsylvania.

11.   iv.   EMMA CLARK CHAMBERS was born on 23 Mar 1875 in Philadelphia, Pennsylvania. She died on 04 Oct 1960 in Newtown Square, Delaware County, Pennsylvania. She married William Young Spence, son of George Spence and Mary Young on 20 Mar 1899 in Delaware County Pennsylvania. He was born on 09 Feb 1871 in Scotland. He died on 31 Dec 1943 in Philadelphia, Pennsylvania.

    v.   ANNIE I. CHAMBERS was born on 12 Feb 1878 in Philadelphia, Pennsylvania. She died on 06 Jan 1944 in Philadelphia, Pennsylvania.

12.   vi.   GEORGE EDWARDS CHAMBERS was born on 01 Jul 1880 in Philadelphia, Pennsylvania. He died on 26 Jun 1937 in Philadelphia, Pennsylvania. He married Annie Richards, daughter of David P. Richards and Susanna Thomas on 24 Apr 1905 in Philadelphia, Pennsylvania. She was born on 05 Jun 1880 in Philadelphia, Pennsylvania. She died on 17 Jan 1953 in Philadelphia, Pennsylvania.

    vii.   ELIZABETH H. CHAMBERS was born on 01 Sep 1883 in Philadelphia, Pennsylvania. She died on 18 Jan 1911 in Philadelphia, Pennsylvania. She married Joseph W. McManus on 16 Apr 1907 in Philadelphia, Pennsylvania. He was born on 17 Sep 1882 in Ireland.

Generation 3

5.   **WILLIAM SCOTT[3] EDWARDS JR.** (William Scott[2], Adam[1]) was born on 13 Jul 1876 in Philadelphia, Pennsylvania. He died on 04 Aug 1949 in Philadelphia, Pennsylvania. He married Gertrude Pierson, daughter of William Pierson and Catherine McCann on 18 Nov 1901 in Delaware. She was born on 13 Feb 1884 in Pennsylvania. She died on 23 Jun 1955 in Philadelphia, Pennsylvania.

William Scott Edwards Jr. and Gertrude Pierson had the following children:

    i.   CATHERINE[4] EDWARDS was born on 12 Aug 1902 in Philadelphia, Pennsylvania. She died on 02 Nov 1948 in Yeadon, Delaware County, Pennsylvania. She married John Dennis Melah on 17 May 1934 in DelawareCounty, Pennsylvania. He was born on 27 Dec 1898 in Pennsylvania. He died in Nov 1984 in Sharon Hill, Delaware County, Pennsylvania.

    ii.   MARIE EDWARDS was born on 25 May 1904 in Philadelphia, Pennsylvania. She died on 10 Nov 1906 in Philadelphia, Pennsylvania.

13.　iii.　ROSE VERONICA EDWARDS was born on 11 Oct 1906 in Philadelphia, Pennsylvania. She died on 26 Jul 1965 in Philadelphia, Pennsylvania. She married Howard C. Albright in 1930 in Philadelphia, Philadelphia County, Pennsylvania. He was born in 1905 in Pennsylvania.

　　　iv.　GERTRUDE EDWARDS JR was born on 18 Oct 1908 in Philadelphia, Pennsylvania. She died on 11 Jun 1969 in Paoli, Chester County, Pennsylvania.

14.　v.　JANE RITA "JENNIE" EDWARDS was born on 04 Dec 1910 in Philadelphia, Pennsylvania. She died on 01 May 1994 in Santa Rosa, Sonoma County, California. She married (1) WILLIAM A. GOLDEN, son of James Golden and Ellen Kelly on 19 Jan 1927 in Delaware County Pennsylvania. He was born on 24 Sep 1904 in Philadelphia, Pennsylvania. She married (2) JOHN O'SHEA after 1932.

15.　vi.　MARGARET R. EDWARDS was born on 10 Oct 1912 in Philadelphia, Pennsylvania. She died on 10 Dec 1999 in Ventnor City, Atlantic County, New Jersey. She married Thomas Augustine Campbell on 19 Jul 1941. He was born on 30 Nov 1907. He died on 27 Oct 1998.

　　　vii.　MARY RITA EDWARDS was born on 16 Jan 1916 in Philadelphia, Pennsylvania. She died on 30 Jul 1991 in Sonoma County, California.

　　　viii.　JOHN J. EDWARDS was born on 21 Mar 1919 in Philadelphia, Pennsylvania. He died on 14 Feb 1987 in Burlington County, New Jersey. He married Ethel Cora Smith, daughter of Joseph E. Smith and Anna S. Bihn on 20 Dec 1941 in Delaware County Pennsylvania. She was born on 17 Jul 1920 in Darby, Delaware County, Pennsylvania. She died on 08 Dec 1996 in Sarasota County, Florida.

6.　**ROSE ANN MARIE³ EDWARDS** (William Scott², Adam¹) was born on 20 Aug 1877 in Philadelphia, Pennsylvania. She died on 29 Jan 1946 in Philadelphia, Pennsylvania. She married James Edward Shields, son of Edward Shields and Catharine Maguire on 30 Jul 1900 in Philadelphia, Philadelphia County, Pennsylvania. He was born on 23 Aug 1876 in Philadelphia, Pennsylvania. He died on 25 Dec 1944 in Philadelphia, Pennsylvania.

James Edward Shields and Rose Ann Marie Edwards had the following child:
　　　i.　JAMES J.⁴ SHIELDS was born on 09 Nov 1900 in Philadelphia, Pennsylvania. He died in 1973 in Pennsylvania. He married Edith H. Weymer in 1924 in Philadelphia, Philadelphia County, Pennsylvania. She was born on 13 Feb 1903 in Pennsylvania. She died in 1985 in Pennsylvania.

7.　**THOMAS J.³ EDWARDS** (William Scott², Adam¹) was born on 14 Apr 1879 in Philadelphia, Pennsylvania. He died on 25 Sep 1905 in Philadelphia, Pennsylvania. He married Della M. Brown in 1902 in Philadelphia Pennsylvania. She was born on 26 Feb 1881 in Philadelphia, Pennsylvania. She died in May 1967 in Philadelphia, Pennsylvania.

Thomas J. Edwards and Della M. Brown had the following children:
　　　i.　WILLIAM⁴ BROWN was born on 06 Sep 1902 in Philadelphia, Pennsylvania.

　　　ii.　MARGARET EDWARDS was born in 1905 in Philadelphia, Pennsylvania. She died on 28 Mar 1909 in Philadelphia, Pennsylvania.

8.　**ISABELLA M.³ EDWARDS** (William Scott², Adam¹) was born on 21 Sep 1889 in Philadelphia, Pennsylvania. She died about 1983. She married John A. Dougherty on 02 Jun 1907 in Philadelphia, Philadelphia County, Pennsylvania. He was born on 16 May 1886 in Philadelphia, Pennsylvania. He died between 1910-1920.

John A. Dougherty and Isabella M. Edwards had the following child:

      i.   ANN ELIZABETH[4] DOUGHERTY was born on 23 Dec 1907 in Philadelphia, Pennsylvania. She died on 29 Jun 1910 in Philadelphia, Pennsylvania.

9.   **WILLIAM SCOTT[3] CHAMBERS** (Annie Adam[2] Edwards, Adam[1] Edwards) was born on 05 Jun 1867 in Philadelphia, Pennsylvania. He died on 05 Feb 1950 in Philadelphia, Pennsylvania. He married (1) **SARAH WHITE**, daughter of Richard White and Catharine (--?--) on 01 Feb 1894 in Philadelphia, Pennsylvania. She was born on 15 Oct 1868 in Philadelphia, Pennsylvania. She died on 14 Aug 1894 in Philadelphia, Pennsylvania. He married (2) **JOSEPHINE IRENE REITZE**, daughter of Christopher Reitze and Lucy S. Devlin on 30 Mar 1896 in Philadelphia, Pennsylvania. She was born on 04 Jul 1877 in Philadelphia, Pennsylvania. She died on 03 May 1962 in Philadelphia, Pennsylvania.

William Scott Chambers and Josephine Irene Reitze had the following children:

16.   i.   HENRY GRAFE[4] CHAMBERS was born on 08 Jan 1897 in Philadelphia, Pennsylvania. He died on 11 Nov 1953 in Collingswood, Camden County, New Jersey. He married Mary Ann McCauley, daughter of Thomas McCauley and Mary Ann Wallace on 30 Jul 1918 in Philadelphia, Pennsylvania. She was born on 07 Jul 1892 in Philadelphia, Pennsylvania. She died on 08 Aug 1984 in Burlington Township, Burlington County, New Jersey.

17.   ii.   LUCY ELIZABETH CHAMBERS was born on 11 Mar 1898 in Philadelphia, Pennsylvania. She died on 22 Nov 1918 in Philadelphia, Pennsylvania. She married William Thompson, son of William Thompson and Hester Carrick on 12 Jun 1915 in Elkton, Cecil County, Maryland. He was born on 28 May 1891 in Pennsylvania. He died on 19 Jun 1965 in Philadelphia, Pennsylvania.

10.   **LYDIA E.[3] CHAMBERS** (Annie Adam[2] Edwards, Adam[1] Edwards) was born on 27 Feb 1872 in Philadelphia, Pennsylvania. She died on 19 Feb 1949 in Philadelphia, Pennsylvania. She married (1) **LEONARD H. SMITH** on 25 Aug 1909 in Philadelphia, Pennsylvania. He was born on 13 Jul 1878 in Germany. She married (2) **JOHN J. ROE** in 1916 in Philadelphia, Philadelphia County, Pennsylvania. He was born on 16 May 1865 in New York. He died on 15 Oct 1929 in Philadelphia, Pennsylvania.

Leonard H. Smith and Lydia E. Chambers had the following child:

18.   i.   MARTHA[4] SMITH was born on 16 Oct 1910 in Pennsylvania. She died on 05 Aug 1990 in Pennsylvania. She married JOSEPH W. HASSELL. He was born in 1913 in Pennsylvania.

11.   **EMMA CLARK[3] CHAMBERS** (Annie Adam[2] Edwards, Adam[1] Edwards) was born on 23 Mar 1875 in Philadelphia, Pennsylvania. She died on 04 Oct 1960 in Newtown Square, Delaware County, Pennsylvania. She married William Young Spence, son of George Spence and Mary Young on 20 Mar 1899 in Delaware County Pennsylvania. He was born on 09 Feb 1871 in Scotland. He died on 31 Dec 1943 in Philadelphia, Pennsylvania.

William Young Spence and Emma Clark Chambers had the following children:

19.   i.   PAULINE L.[4] SPENCE was born on 22 Jul 1899 in Philadelphia, Pennsylvania. She died on 17 Dec 1959 in Philadelphia, Pennsylvania. She married WILLIAM FREDERICK GURK SR.. He was born on 21 Sep 1897 in Philadelphia, Pennsylvania. He died on 20 Jan 1981 in Hartford, Hartford County, Connecticut.

      ii.   LYDIA VIOLA SPENCE was born on 09 Jun 1902 in Pennsylvania. She died on 21 Aug 1989 in Lee County Florida. She married George Clemens Enge in 1928 in Philadelphia, Pennsylvania. He was born on 17 Aug 1900 in Pennsylvania. He died on 26 Dec 1987 in Collier County Florida.

20.   iii.   WILLIAM YOUNG SPENCE JR. was born on 12 Nov 1904 in Philadelphia, Pennsylvania. He died on 29 Jan 1954 in Philadelphia Pennsylvania. He married Mae A. Prescott, daughter of father Prescott and Freda A on 05 Aug 1938 in Delaware County Pennsylvania. She was born in 1913 in Pennsylvania.

         iv.   GEORGE E. SPENCE was born on 09 Jun 1908 in Pennsylvania. He died on 14 May 1983 in Stone Harbor, Cape May County, New Jersey. He married Marie E. Priggemeier on 17 Jun 1938 in Philadelphia, Pennsylvania. She was born on 24 May 1909 in Pennsylvania. She died on 19 Sep 2002 in Stone Harbor, Cape May County, New Jersey.

12.   **GEORGE EDWARDS³ CHAMBERS** (Annie Adam² Edwards, Adam¹ Edwards) was born on 01 Jul 1880 in Philadelphia, Pennsylvania. He died on 26 Jun 1937 in Philadelphia, Pennsylvania. He married Annie Richards, daughter of David P. Richards and Susanna Thomas on 24 Apr 1905 in Philadelphia, Pennsylvania. She was born on 05 Jun 1880 in Philadelphia, Pennsylvania. She died on 17 Jan 1953 in Philadelphia, Pennsylvania.

George Edwards Chambers and Annie Richards had the following children:

         i.   ANNIE⁴ CHAMBERS was born on 24 Jun 1907 in Philadelphia, Pennsylvania. She died on 24 Jun 1907 in Philadelphia, Pennsylvania.

21.   ii.   GEORGE RICHARDS CHAMBERS SR. was born on 14 Sep 1908 in Philadelphia, Pennsylvania. He died on 29 Sep 1984 in Philadelphia, Pennsylvania. He married Mary Luciano in 1934 in Philadelphia, Philadelphia County, Pennsylvania. She was born on 24 Aug 1913 in Philadelphia, Pennsylvania. She died on 24 Jan 1979 in Philadelphia, Pennsylvania.

         iii.   GERTRUDE HELEN CHAMBERS was born in Dec 1910 in Washington, D.C.. She died on 18 Mar 1911 in Washington, D.C..

Generation 4

13.   **ROSE VERONICA⁴ EDWARDS** (William Scott³ Jr., William Scott², Adam¹) was born on 11 Oct 1906 in Philadelphia, Pennsylvania. She died on 26 Jul 1965 in Philadelphia, Pennsylvania. She married Howard C. Albright in 1930 in Philadelphia, Philadelphia County, Pennsylvania. He was born in 1905 in Pennsylvania.

Howard C. Albright and Rose Veronica Edwards had the following children:

         i.   HOWARD J.⁵ ALBRIGHT was born in 1938 in Pennsylvania. He married Margaret Harkins on 22 Oct 1960. She was born on 15 Jul 1937. She died on 25 Dec 2011.

         ii.   KATHRYN R. ALBRIGHT was born on 29 Jan 1943. She married Dennis Green on 25 Jun 1966 in Philadelphia, Pennsylvania. He was born on 22 Sep 1941 in Berks County, Pennsyvania. He died on 12 Sep 2012 in Berks County, Pennsylvania.

14.   **JANE RITA "JENNIE"⁴ EDWARDS** (William Scott³ Jr., William Scott², Adam¹) was born on 04 Dec 1910 in Philadelphia, Pennsylvania. She died on 01 May 1994 in Santa Rosa, Sonoma County, California. She married (1) **WILLIAM A. GOLDEN**, son of James Golden and Ellen Kelly on 19 Jan 1927 in Delaware County Pennsylvania. He was born on 24 Sep 1904 in Philadelphia, Pennsylvania. She married (2) **JOHN O'SHEA** after 1932.

William A. Golden and Jane Rita "Jennie" Edwards had the following children:

         i.   WILLIAM⁵ GOLDEN JR. was born in Apr 1928 in Philadelphia, Pennsylvania. He died on 23 Aug 1928 in Philadelphia, Pennsylvania.

         ii.   JOHN JOSEPH GOLDEN was born on 01 Oct 1929 in Philadelphia, Pennsylvania. He died on 16 Oct 1982 in Los Angeles County, California.

    iii.   EDWARD A. GOLDEN was born on 20 Oct 1931 in Philadelphia, Pennsylvania. He died on 12 Sep 1999 in Peoria, Peoria County, Illinois.

    iv.   JAMES J. GOLDEN was born on 12 Nov 1932 in Philadelphia, Pennsylvania. He died on 26 May 2005 in Lester, Delaware County, Pennsylvania..

15.   MARGARET R.⁴ EDWARDS (William Scott³ Jr., William Scott², Adam¹) was born on 10 Oct 1912 in Philadelphia, Pennsylvania. She died on 10 Dec 1999 in Ventnor City, Atlantic County, New Jersey. She married Thomas Augustine Campbell on 19 Jul 1941. He was born on 30 Nov 1907. He died on 27 Oct 1998.

Thomas Augustine Campbell and Margaret R. Edwards had the following children:
    i.   ANNE M.⁵ CAMPBELL was born on 16 Sep 1942.

    ii.   THOMAS A. CAMPBELL. He married DONNA.

16.   HENRY GRAFE⁴ CHAMBERS (William Scott³, Annie Adam² Edwards, Adam¹ Edwards) was born on 08 Jan 1897 in Philadelphia, Pennsylvania. He died on 11 Nov 1953 in Collingswood, Camden County, New Jersey. He married Mary Ann McCauley, daughter of Thomas McCauley and Mary Ann Wallace on 30 Jul 1918 in Philadelphia, Pennsylvania. She was born on 07 Jul 1892 in Philadelphia, Pennsylvania. She died on 08 Aug 1984 in Burlington Township, Burlington County, New Jersey.

Henry Grafe Chambers and Mary Ann McCauley had the following children:
    i.   WILLIAM SCOTT⁵ CHAMBERS was born on 25 Feb 1921 in Philadelphia, Pennsylvania. He died on 08 Feb 2014 in Plantation Broward County Florida. He married Gloria Ann Freda, daughter of Guerino Angelo Maria Freda and Filomena M. Quaresima on 26 Jan 1946 in Princeton, Mercer County, New Jersey. She was born on 06 Mar 1921 in Princeton, Mercer County, New Jersey. She died on 28 Aug 1987 in Portsmouth, Virginia.

    ii.   THOMAS WALLACE CHAMBERS was born on 25 Mar 1923 in Philadelphia, Pennsylvania. He died on 06 Oct 1955 in Stateburg, Sumter County, South Carolina. He married Florence Clark, daughter of James Freeman Clark and Anna Lee on 31 May 1948 in New Castle, New Castle County, Delaware. She was born on 13 Apr 1930 in Haddonfield, Camden County, New Jersey. She died on 16 Feb 2016 in Churchville, Bucks County, Pennsylvania.

17.   LUCY ELIZABETH⁴ CHAMBERS (William Scott³, Annie Adam² Edwards, Adam¹ Edwards) was born on 11 Mar 1898 in Philadelphia, Pennsylvania. She died on 22 Nov 1918 in Philadelphia, Pennsylvania. She married William Thompson, son of William Thompson and Hester Carrick on 12 Jun 1915 in Elkton, Cecil County, Maryland. He was born on 28 May 1891 in Pennsylvania. He died on 19 Jun 1965 in Philadelphia, Pennsylvania.

William Thompson and Lucy Elizabeth Chambers had the following child:
    i.   JOSEPHINE HESTER⁵ THOMPSON was born on 10 May 1916 in Philadelphia, Pennsylvania. She died on 06 Oct 2008 in Haddonfield, Camden County, New Jersey. She married David Harrington Marshall Sr., son of Thomas Marshall on 13 Jun 1942 in Philadelphia, Pennsylvania. He was born on 27 Jun 1912 in Philadelphia, Pennsylvania. He died on 02 Nov 2009 in Newark, Delaware.

18.   MARTHA⁴ SMITH (Lydia E.³ Chambers, Annie Adam² Edwards, Adam¹ Edwards) was born on 16 Oct 1910 in Pennsylvania. She died on 05 Aug 1990 in Pennsylvania. She married JOSEPH W.

HASSELL. He was born in 1913 in Pennsylvania.

Joseph W. Hassell and Martha Smith had the following child:

     i.   JOSEPH WILLIAM[5] HASSELL JR. was born on 22 Jun 1935 in Philadelphia, Pennsylvania. He died on 29 Sep 2006 in Philadelphia, Pennsylvania.

19.   **PAULINE L.[4] SPENCE** (Emma Clark[3] Chambers, Annie Adam[2] Edwards, Adam[1] Edwards) was born on 22 Jul 1899 in Philadelphia, Pennsylvania. She died on 17 Dec 1959 in Philadelphia, Pennsylvania. She married **WILLIAM FREDERICK GURK SR.**. He was born on 21 Sep 1897 in Philadelphia, Pennsylvania. He died on 20 Jan 1981 in Hartford, Hartford County, Connecticut.

William Frederick Gurk Sr. and Pauline L. Spence had the following child:

     i.   WILLIAM FREDERICK[5] GURK JR. was born on 04 Feb 1919 in Philadelphia, Pennsylvania. He died on 27 Sep 2010 in Philadelphia, Pennsylvania. He married Gertrude E. Murtagh in 1945 in Philadelphia, Pennsylvania. She was born about 1924.

20.   **WILLIAM YOUNG[4] SPENCE JR.** (Emma Clark[3] Chambers, Annie Adam[2] Edwards, Adam[1] Edwards) was born on 12 Nov 1904 in Philadelphia, Pennsylvania. He died on 29 Jan 1954 in Philadelphia Pennsylvania. He married Mae A. Prescott, daughter of father Prescott and Freda A on 05 Aug 1938 in Delaware County Pennsylvania. She was born in 1913 in Pennsylvania.

William Young Spence Jr. and Mae A. Prescott had the following child:

     i.   WILLIAM "BILLY"[5] SPENCE was born about 1939.

21.   **GEORGE RICHARDS[4] CHAMBERS SR.** (George Edwards[3], Annie Adam[2] Edwards, Adam[1] Edwards) was born on 14 Sep 1908 in Philadelphia, Pennsylvania. He died on 29 Sep 1984 in Philadelphia, Pennsylvania. He married Mary Luciano in 1934 in Philadelphia, Philadelphia County, Pennsylvania. She was born on 24 Aug 1913 in Philadelphia, Pennsylvania. She died on 24 Jan 1979 in Philadelphia, Pennsylvania.

George Richards Chambers Sr. and Mary Luciano had the following children:

     i.   GEORGE RICHARDS[5] CHAMBERS JR. was born on 25 Jul 1934 in Philadelphia, Pennsylvania. He married (1) RUTH KEPHARDT about 1958. He married (2) LOIS K. LAFFERTY, daughter of Harry Lafferty and Lydia Helen Butterfield on 06 Nov 1977. She was born on 06 Mar 1933. She died on 21 Feb 2003 in Pennsylvania.

     ii.   DOROTHY ANNA CHAMBERS was born on 12 Jan 1936 in Philadelphia, Pennsylvania. She died on 17 Jul 2012 in Newark, New Castle County, Delaware. She married Alton Lamar Brooks on 03 Mar 1956. He was born on 03 Sep 1930. He died on 31 Jan 1993 in Delaware.

     iii.   JOSEPH D. CHAMBERS SR. was born on 30 Dec 1936 in Philadelphia, Pennsylvania. He died on 03 May 2013 in Wilmington, Delaware. He married Joan F. Walker on 24 Jan 1964 in Collingdale, Delaware County Pennsylvania. She was born on 04 Apr 1932 in Pennsylvania.

(–?–), Ann, 28,29
(–?–), Caroline, 20
(–?–), Mary, 21
Adam, Agnes, 4,5
Adam, John, 4,5
Brown, Anne, 1,2,3
Brown, Susan, 16,17
Chambers, Annie, 33,34
Chambers, Annie Adam (Edwards),
1,5,7,8,9,10,11,12,15,17,28,29,30,31,32,33,
34,35
Chambers, Eliza Jane, 32,33,34
Chambers, Elizabeth "Bessie", 33,34
Chambers, Emma, 32,33,34
Chambers, George Edwards, 33,34
Chambers, George Washington,
21,29,31,32,33,34,35
Chambers, Henry Grafe, 34
Chambers, Josephine (Reitze), 35
Chambers, Lucy, 34
Chambers, Lydia, 33
Chambers, William Scott, 32,33,35
Clark, Ann (–?–), 29
Clark, Emma (Chambers), 32,33
Clark, John, 29,32,33
Clark, Rose, 28,29,30
Clark, Thomas, 29
Cook, William, 17
Cusack, Elizabeth "Lizzie", 13,20,28
Dougherty, Edward,21
Dougherty, James, 21
Dougherty, John, 21
Dougherty, Mary, 21
Dougherty, Mary (–?–), 21
Dougherty, Thomas, 21
Durborrow, George A. (Reverend), 16,20,31
Edwards, Adam, 1,4,5,6,7,8,9,10,11,15,17
Edwards, Agnes (Adam), 4,5
Edwards, Alexander, 1,4,5,6,8,9,10
Edwards, Ann, 5,8
Edwards, Annie Adam,
1,5,7,8,9,10,11,12,13,15,17,28,29,30,31,32,

33,34,35
Edwards, Bella, 21,22
Edwards, Elizabeth "Lizzie" (Cusack),
13,20,28
Edwards, George,
1,4,5,6,7,8,9,10,11,12,13,15,16,
17,20,22,28,32,33
Edwards, Isabella (Scott),
1,2,3,4,6,7,9,10,11,12,13,14,15,17,20,21,22,
25,32,34
Edwards, Jane, 5
Edwards, Jane (Martin), 14,27,28
Edwards, Joseph Campbell, 1,7,10,11,32
Edwards, Margaret, 10
Edwards, Margaret (McIntosh), 4,5,9,10
Edwards, Mary (–?–) Dougherty, 21
Edwards, Peter, 9,10
Edwards, Robert,
1,5,7,9,10,11,12,13,17,18,19,20,21,28,32,34
Edwards, Robert Hunter,
1,5,7,9,10,11,12,13,17,18,19,20,21,28,32,34
Edwards, Rose Ann (McFeely), 20, 21
Edwards, Rose (Clark), 28,29,30
Edwards, Susan, 5
Edwards, Susan (Brown), 16,17
Edwards, Thomas, 30
Edwards, William Joseph, see William Scott
Edwards
Edwards, William Scott,
1,7,8,9,10,11,12,14,15,21,22,23,24,25,26,27,
28,29,30,32,34
Flanagan, Andrew, 12,13,14,15,22,28,30,32
Flanagan, Isabella (Scott) Edwards,
1,2,3,4,6,7,9,10,11,12,13,14,15,17,20,21,22,
25,32,34
Feely, Rose Ann, see McFeely
Freed, John, 28,32
Kelly, Alexander, 12,27
Lamb, Ann (–?–) Martin, 28
Leacock, George, 15
Liggett, Samuel, 17
Marden, Jane, see Martin

INDEX

Marshall, Josephine (Thompson), 30,33,35

Martin, Ann (–?–), 28

Martin, Jane, 14,27,28

Martin, William J., 28

McFarland, James, 7

McFeely, Rose Ann, 20, 21

McIntosh, Margaret, 4,5,6,9,10

McIntosh, Peter, 4

McManus, Elizabeth "Bessie" Chambers, 33,34

Moses, Nathan (Captain), 8

Proctor, George, 12

Reitze, Josephine, 35

Roundtree, James, 17

Rountree, James, see Roundtree

Rountree, William, 13

Scott, Andrew, 3

Scott, Anne (Brown), 1,2,3

Scott, Isabella, 1,2,3,4,6,7,9,10,11,12,13,14,15,17,20,21,22, 25,32,34

Scott, William, 1,2,3,4

Spence, Emma (Chambers), 32,33,34

Thompson, Josephine, 30,33,35

Thompson, Lucy (Chambers), 34

Watson, G. (Doctor), 9,10

Young, Caroline (–?–), 20

Young, Henry, 20

Young, Mary, 20